great **salads** and **sides**

great salads and sides

simply delicious recipes for everyday eating and entertaining

fiona smith

photography by diana miller

RYLAND
PETERS
& SMALL
LONDON NEW YORK

Dedication
For my mother, Naomi Roydhouse.

Senior Designer Toni Kay
Commissioning Editor Julia Charles
Production Controller Hazel Kirkman
Art Director Leslie Harrington
Publishing Director Alison Starling

Food Stylist Valerie Berry
Prop Stylist Wei Tang
Index Hilary Bird

Author's acknowledgements
Thanks to all my family and friends,
always there with encouragement
and empty plates.

First published in the United Kingdom
in 2009 by Ryland Peters & Small
20–21 Jockey's Fields
London WC1R 4BW
www.rylandpeters.com

10 9 8 7 6 5 4 3 2 1

ISBN: 978 1 84597 836 5

A CIP record for this book is available
from the British Library.

Printed in China

Notes
• All spoon measurements are level
unless otherwise specified.
• Herbs used in the recipes are fresh
unless specified as dried.
• When a recipe calls for the zest of
lemons or limes, buy unwaxed fruit and
wash well before using. If you can only
find treated fruit, scrub well in warm
soapy water and rinse before using.
• Raw or partially cooked eggs should
not be served to the very young or old,
to pregnant women or to anyone with
a compromised immune system.
• Ovens should be preheated to the
specified temperature. If using a fan-
assisted oven, follow the manufacturer's
instructions for adjusting temperatures.
• Always sterilize preserving jars before
use. See note on page 127.

contents

introduction

Good food often needs no other adornment except perhaps a little sprinkle of
salt and pepper, a squeeze of fresh lemon juice or a drizzle of extra virgin olive oil.
If you buy a perfect piece of steak or fish, you don't want to mask its flavour by
cooking it in complicated ways. Simple preparations such as barbecuing, grilling,
steaming and poaching are usually enough for fine cuts (save the slow cooking for
the lesser cuts). But to make it a meal, you need a good recipe that will complement
it. Accompaniments such as salads, warm side dishes, salsas and sauces can add
balance, flavour, colour and texture to simple foods and make a complete meal.

When choosing accompaniments, consider what you are serving them with; they
should enhance rather than overpower other elements of the meal. For a barbecue
buffet, you may want a selection of salads and sides – choose combinations such
as one leafy salad, one carb-based side and one warm vegetable dish rather than
three that are carb-based or all hot. Take into account the texture and the look of
each dish – a spread of green sides is less appealing than a variety of colours.
What you are serving the dishes with is important as well. With simply barbecued
food many recipes will work, but some are better than others – chicken and fish
are terrific with spicy or fruity sides; steak possibly not so. I have given serving
suggestions throughout the book where I think certain combinations work best.

While most of the recipes in this book are designed as accompaniments to add to
a meal (and perfect for those occasions where you are asked to 'bring a plate'),
I have also included a chapter on main course salads. These are heartier and more
balanced as a whole, and will satisfy the appetite on their own. I also often use a

green salad as a base for a more substantial meal. For example, simply adding some finely sliced pears and cubed blue cheese or Parmesan shavings creates an exciting new dish. You can add whatever fresh vegetables you have along with tinned tuna, crumbled feta cheese or crisp bacon pieces to make a easy, healthy midweek dinner that's quick and simple to prepare.

A recipe is often just a starting point for many cooks, who go on to add, subtract and adapt it to suit their own tastes and available ingredients. These recipes are perfect for that, because unlike something like baking, changing ingredients a little shouldn't drastically affect the outcome. Make the most of seasonal produce, especially vegetables that come packed with flavour when in season. Salads and side dishes are the perfect way to get lots of healthy vegetables into your diet, so also consider a balance of colours: red, green, yellow, orange, white, brown and purple. As the Western world redefines its diet for health reasons, increasing consumption of fruit, vegetables and pulses, and reducing fats and meat portions, it makes sense to borrow from those who have cooked this way throughout history. There are so many interesting international foods now available that make great additions to a salad or side. I like to make good use of more unusual ingredients, such as preserved lemons and pomegranate molasses, as they add fabulous depth of flavour. When you have tried a recipe with an ingredient such as pomegranate molasses, its addictive sweet-and-sour fruitiness will inspire you to experiment by adding it to other dishes. Stirring in finely chopped preserved lemon rind can turn a plain potato salad into something with real wow factor. I have included a glossary of my favourite ingredients (see pages 140–141) to enable you to make the most of them. You'll also find some suggested retailers listed on page 144 to help you source those that your local supermarket or deli may not yet stock. I do hope my recipes induce you to try some fresh new tastes and flavour experiences.

side salads

classic green salad

150 g crisp lettuce, such as cos or iceberg

100 g soft leaf lettuce, such as butterhead or lamb's lettuce

75 g peppery salad leaves, such as rocket or watercress OR bitter leaves, such as frisée, with radicchio for added colour

classic vinaigrette

1 teaspoon Dijon mustard

¼ teaspoon sea salt

⅛ teaspoon freshly ground black pepper

1 tablespoon white wine vinegar

3 tablespoons extra virgin olive oil

SERVES 4

Simple and elegant, fresh and vibrant tasting, a classic green salad is the perfect accompaniment to any meal. It can be served before, during or after the main course.

Wash and thoroughly dry all the salad leaves. Tear any very large leaves into bite-sized pieces. To make the classic vinaigrette, whisk together the mustard, salt, pepper and vinegar in a large salad bowl until combined. Whisk in the olive oil. Just before serving, toss the leaves through the dressing. Serve immediately.

Variations:

Fresh soft herbs such as basil, tarragon, chervil, mint and chives can be added to give flavour. Match the herb to the meal you are having. For example, tarragon goes very well with chicken; chervil with fish; basil with Mediterranean-style dishes; and mint with lamb.

The type of vinegar you use can also subtly change the flavour of the salad dressing. Try cider, balsamic, rice wine or a herb-infused vinegar such as tarragon. If you prefer your salad dressing to have a less acidic taste, simply add 2 teaspoons runny honey.

pea, prosciutto and pasta salad

350 g pasta shape of your choice, such as orecchiette, fusilli or farfalle

1 tablespoon olive oil

1 large onion, finely chopped

2 garlic cloves, crushed

100 g sliced prosciutto or bacon rashers

350 g frozen or fresh peas

2 tablespoons extra virgin olive oil

2 tablespoons white wine vinegar

1 teaspoon Dijon mustard

2 tablespoons chopped parsley

2 tablespoons chopped chervil

2 tablespoons chopped mint

sea salt and freshly ground black pepper

SERVES 6

This is an elegant and light twist on a traditional pasta salad. You can either use frozen peas or make the most of the tender sweetness of fresh peas when they are in season; as a rule of thumb, 500 g pea pods will yield about 175 g fresh peas.

Bring a large saucepan of water to the boil, add plenty of salt and return to the boil. Cook the pasta according to the packet instructions.

While the pasta is cooking, heat the olive oil in a frying pan set over medium heat. Add the onion and garlic and cook for 5 minutes. Add the prosciutto and cook a further 5 minutes. Add the peas, cover and cook gently for 5 minutes until the peas are tender. (Remember that fresh peas will need slightly less cooking time.)

In a bowl, mix together the extra virgin olive oil, vinegar and mustard, adding salt and pepper to taste.

When the pasta is cooked, drain and refresh with cold water to cool a little. Combine the pasta with the pea and prosciutto mixture, vinaigrette, parsley, chervil and mint.

2 corn-on-the-cob, husked

4 large, ripe tomatoes,
cut into wedges

400-g jar or tin artichoke
hearts, drained

1 tablespoon white
wine vinegar

3 tablespoons olive or
avocado oil

leaves from a large bunch
of basil

sea salt flakes and freshly
ground black pepper

polenta-crumbed aubergine

2 small aubergines

1 egg

1 tablespoon milk

90 g instant polenta

1 teaspoon cumin seeds,
lightly crushed

2 tablespoons chopped thyme
or ½ teaspoon dried

30 g plain flour

½ teaspoon sea salt

2 tablespoons avocado or
olive oil

SERVES 4

Sweetcorn and tomatoes are seasonal vegetables that really are much better in the summertime. I like to dress them very simply so their flavour shines through. Polenta makes a terrific instant crumb for vegetables, adding crunch and a subtle corn flavour.

summer vegetables
with polenta-crumbed aubergine

Bring a large saucepan of water to the boil and add the corn-on-the-cobs. Cook for 8 minutes or until tender when pierced with a knife. Drain and set aside to cool.

Cut the kernels off the cobs, trying to keep the corn kernels in large pieces. Arrange the corn on a plate with the tomatoes and artichoke hearts. Drizzle over the vinegar and oil and season to taste with salt and pepper.

To make the polenta-crumbed aubergine, slice the aubergines into slices 1 cm thick. Beat the egg together with the milk and put in a shallow dish. In a separate dish, combine the polenta, cumin and thyme. Put the flour and salt in a third dish.

Heat the oil in a large frying pan set over medium heat. Dip each slice of aubergine first in the flour, then the egg and milk mixture and finally into the polenta. Fry for 3 minutes on each side until golden and cooked through. Arrange the polenta-crumbed aubergine on top of the prepared summer vegetables and garnish with the basil leaves to serve.

asparagus, mangetout and fennel salad with goats' cheese dressing

500 g asparagus, trimmed

250 g mangetout, sliced lengthways

2 large fennel bulbs, with fronds

goats' cheese dressing

100 g soft goats' cheese

3–4 tablespoons verjuice* or freshly squeezed lemon juice

4 tablespoon olive oil

sea salt and freshly ground black pepper

micro greens*, to garnish (optional)

SERVES 6

*see glossary pages 140–141

Here a fresh green salad is given a twist with a tangy goats' cheese dressing. You will need to use a soft, creamy cheese for a smooth, pourable result. Serve as an accompaniment to grilled vegetables, chicken, lamb or smoked fish or meat.

Bring a saucepan of water to the boil, add the asparagus and cook until tender. Drain and refresh with cold water. (Alternatively, you can grill the asparagus on the barbecue.) Cut the asparagus into pieces 5 cm long. Put in a bowl and set aside.

Bring a saucepan of water to the boil and add the mangetout. Drain immediately and refresh with cold water. Add to the cooked asparagus.

Remove the fronds from the fennel, chop and set aside. Finely shave the fennel bulb, using a mandoline if you have one, or cut as finely as possible with a sharp knife. Add to the asparagus and mangetout along with the fennel fronds. Cover and chill until needed.

To make the goats' cheese dressing, mash the cheese with a fork in a small bowl. Stir in 3 tablespoons of the verjuice and whisk in the oil. If the dressing is too thick, add a little more verjuice until it is the desired consistency. Season to taste with salt and pepper.

Combine the asparagus, mangetout and fennel with the dressing just before serving and garnish with a sprinkling of micro greens, if using.

This is a combination of two styles of courgette, one marinated and grilled for a deep flavour and soft texture, the other very finely sliced and marinated for a crunchy texture and fresh flavour.

double courgette, parmesan and walnut salad

3 tablespoons freshly squeezed lemon juice

finely grated zest of 2 lemons

½ teaspoon sea salt

6 tablespoons extra virgin olive oil

12 small or 24 baby courgettes

6 medium courgettes

70 g walnuts, toasted

leaves from a small bunch of basil or mint, chopped

50 g Parmesan cheese shavings

freshly ground black pepper

SERVES 6

To make the marinade, whisk together the lemon juice and zest with the salt and ¼ teaspoon black pepper in a small bowl, then slowly whisk in the oil.

Slice the small courgettes as thinly as possible, using a mandoline if you have one. Put in a shallow, non-reactive dish and pour over half the marinade. Cover and leave to marinate at room temperature for at least 1 hour and up to 6 hours, turning occasionally.

Thickly slice the medium courgettes and put them in another shallow, non-reactive dish. Pour over the remaining marinade, cover and leave to marinate at room temperature for 1 hour.

Heat a barbecue or grill until hot and cook the medium courgettes for 1–2 minutes on each side. Let cool. Arrange both the marinated and grilled courgettes together on a serving dish and scatter over the walnuts and basil. Finish with shavings of Parmesan and freshly ground black pepper.

90 g bulghur wheat

2 spring onions, finely chopped

1 celery stick, finely chopped

1 red pepper, deseeded and
finely chopped

1 green apple, cored and
finely chopped

cider mayonnaise

1 tablespoon grainy mustard

1 tablespoon apple syrup* or
runny honey

2 tablespoons cider vinegar

2 tablespoons mayonnaise

a large bunch of flat leaf
parsley, stems removed

freshly ground black pepper

SERVES 4–6

see glossary pages 140–141

green apple and wheat salad
with cider mayonnaise

Bulghur wheat-based salads such as tabbouleh are quick, easy
and substantial. You could also substitute another grain, such
as barley, cooked according to the packet instructions.

Put the bulghur wheat in a bowl and cover with cold water. Leave to
soak for 30 minutes until tender but not too soft. Drain well and press
down hard on the bulghur wheat with the back of a spoon to squeeze
out excess water.

Put the bulghur wheat in a salad bowl with the spring onions, celery,
red pepper and apple.

To make the cider mayonnaise, whisk together the mustard, apple syrup,
vinegar and mayonnaise in a small bowl and add black pepper to taste.
Add this to the bulghur mixture, cover and refrigerate until needed.

Remove the salad from the refrigerator about 30 minutes before serving
and bring to room temperature. Stir in the chopped parsley to serve.

150 g quinoa*

1 small red onion

rind of 1 preserved lemon*, finely chopped, OR finely grated zest of 1 fresh lemon

75 g rocket

a large bunch of flat leaf parsley, stems removed

a small bunch of mint, chopped

a handful of chives, chopped

freshly squeezed juice of 1 lemon

¼ teaspoon ground cinnamon

4 tablespoons extra virgin olive oil

sea salt and freshly ground black pepper

SERVES 6

see glossary pages 140–141

herb, red onion and quinoa salad with preserved lemon

This refreshing salad is packed with green herbs and has a light touch of spice. It makes the perfect accompaniment to salmon, poultry, pork and lamb.

Bring a medium saucepan of salted water to the boil. Rinse the quinoa in a sieve under cold running water, then add to the boiling water. Cook for 12–15 minutes until tender. Drain and let cool.

Slice the onion very finely, using a mandoline if you have one. Put in a bowl of iced water for 10 minutes. Drain well.

In a bowl, combine the quinoa, onion, preserved lemon rind, rocket, parsley, mint and chives.

In a small bowl, whisk together the lemon juice, cinnamon and ¼ teaspoon each of salt and pepper. Whisk in the oil.

Toss the salad and dressing together just before serving.

This Japanese-inspired salad involves cooking the beans twice. The first cooking allows the green colour of the beans to be set as well as cooking the beans evenly while still retaining a crunch. The second gives the beans more depth of flavour.

green bean and chickpea salad
with sesame dressing

450 g green beans

2 tablespoons sake*
or dry sherry

3 teaspoons sugar

5 teaspoons Japanese
soy sauce*

240 ml fish or vegetable stock

40 g sesame seeds

410-g tin chickpeas, drained

½ teaspoon sesame oil

SERVES 6

*see glossary pages 140–141

Bring a saucepan of water to the boil, add the beans and cook for 5 minutes until bright green and tender but still firm to the bite. Drain and rinse in cold water, then plunge into iced water to set their colour.

Bring the sake to the boil in a small saucepan and then transfer to a bowl and combine with the sugar and soy sauce.

Put the stock in a saucepan with 1 tablespoon of the sake mixture. Bring to the boil. Drain the beans and add to the stock. Return to the boil, then remove from the heat, drain and let cool.

Heat a frying pan until hot, add the sesame seeds and toast, tossing them in the pan constantly, until they are golden. Transfer the toasted seeds to a mortar and pestle, mini food processor or spice grinder and grind them to a rough paste.

In a bowl, combine the ground sesame seeds with the chickpeas, oil and the remaining sake mixture, then toss through the drained beans. Serve immediately.

I like to make the most of avocados when they are in season. This salad makes a tasty addition to a Mexican dish, but also goes well with the smoky flavours of any barbecued meat or fish.

tomato, avocado and lime salad
with crisp tortillas

freshly squeezed juice of
1 lime, plus 1 lime

4 ripe, firm avocados

leaves from a large bunch
of coriander

24 small tomatoes, halved

6 tablespoons olive or
avocado oil

2 garlic cloves, crushed

2 flour tortillas

sea salt and freshly ground
black pepper

SERVES 6

Put the lime juice in a bowl. Cut the avocados in half, remove the stones and peel. Cut each half into 4 wedges and toss with the lime juice.

Using a small paring knife, cut the top and bottom off of the lime. Cut away the skin and pith. Carefully slice between each segment and remove the flesh. Combine the lime flesh with the avocados, coriander, tomatoes and 4 tablespoons of the oil. Season to taste with salt and pepper and set aside.

Preheat the grill to hot.

In a small bowl, combine the garlic and remaining 2 tablespoons of oil. Brush the oil and garlic mixture over the tortillas and toast under the preheated grill for about 1 minute until brown.

Break the toasted tortillas into pieces and scatter over the salad just before serving.

A sweet, light, fresh salad, perfect with shellfish, fish or poultry. The orange chipotle vinaigrette also make a tasty dressing for pan-fried prawns.

melon, cos and cucumber salad
with orange chipotle vinaigrette

125 g baby cos lettuce leaves

400 g canteloupe melon

400 g honeydew melon

400 g watermelon

1 small (Lebanese) cucumber

a small bunch of coriander

orange chipotle vinaigrette

4 tablespoons olive oil

1 chipotle chilli or 2 fresh mild red chillies plus ¼ teaspoon smoked paprika

1 tablespoon sherry vinegar or cider vinegar

finely grated zest and freshly squeezed juice of 1 orange

1 tablespoon runny honey

1 teaspoon sea salt

SERVES 4-6

Arrange the cos lettuce on a large serving platter. Remove and discard the skin and seeds from the melons and slice the flesh into slices 1 cm thick. Arrange these over the cos lettuce. Halve the cucumber lengthways and remove and discard the seeds. Slice thinly and arrange over the melon.

To make the chipotle vinaigrette, heat 1 teaspoon of the olive oil in a frying pan, add the chipotle chilli and briefly sauté for 2 minutes, stirring constantly, taking care not to let it burn.

Using kitchen scissors or a sharp knife, remove the stem and seeds (leave the seeds in for extra heat if liked) from the chipotle and discard. Cut the chipotle into thin strips. If using fresh chillies, remove the stem and seeds and discard, then chop the chillies finely.

In a bowl, whisk together the vinegar, orange zest and juice, honey, salt and remaining olive oil. Add the prepared chillies and stir to combine.

Pour the vinaigrette over the cos, melon and cucumber on the serving platter, scatter with coriander sprigs and serve immediately.

200 g rice stick noodles*

1 tablespoon groundnut oil

3 carrots, peeled

200 g Savoy or Chinese
cabbage, very thinly sliced

6 radishes, thinly sliced

3 spring onions, thinly
sliced lengthways

100 g water chestnuts,
thinly sliced

70 g cashew nuts or almonds,
toasted and roughly chopped

Chinese five-spice dressing

1 tablespoon sugar

½ teaspoon crushed fresh
red chilli

½ teaspoon Chinese
five-spice powder*

2 tablespoons Japanese
soy sauce*

2 tablespoons rice vinegar*

1 tablespoon freshly squeezed
lime or lemon juice

1 teaspoon sesame oil

SERVES 6

*see glossary pages 140–141

rice noodle, carrot and cabbage salad with chinese five-spice dressing

This is a spicy twist on coleslaw. To turn it into a substantial meal, simply toss through cooked and sliced chicken or pork or fried tofu.

Put the rice stick noodles in a heatproof bowl and cover with boiling water. Leave for 5 minutes or until soft, then drain well. Toss with the groundnut oil to stop the noodles sticking together.

To make the Chinese five-spice dressing, combine the sugar, chilli, five-spice powder, soy sauce, vinegar, lime juice and sesame oil in a small bowl. Stir until the sugar has dissolved.

Cut the carrots into thin ribbons – this can be done using a mandoline if you have one or a vegetable peeler. Put in a large bowl with the noodles, cabbage, radishes, spring onions and water chestnuts. Add the dressing and toss to mix.

Transfer to a serving dish and scatter with the toasted nuts to serve.

Broccoli is sturdy enough to handle strong flavours and makes a great end of summer salad that is hearty yet still fresh. If you are a fan of cauliflower, you can substitute it for the broccoli.

broccoli and grilled pepper salad
with caper and anchovy dressing

4 medium red and/or orange peppers

1 head of broccoli, about 350 g

50 g pine nuts

150 g rashers of bacon

1–2 mild red chillies, thinly sliced

2 tablespoons olive oil

30 g fresh breadcrumbs

2 garlic cloves, thinly sliced

caper and anchovy dressing

1 teaspoon sugar

3 tablespoons drained capers

8 anchovy fillets, finely chopped

freshly squeezed juice of 1 lemon

1 tablespoon white wine vinegar or sherry vinegar

4 tablespoons extra virgin olive oil

sea salt and freshly ground black pepper

SERVES 6

Preheat the grill to very hot.

Cut the peppers in half and arrange cut-side down on a baking tray. Put under the grill and cook for about 10 minutes, until the skins are blackened. Transfer the peppers to a bowl, cover the bowl with clingfilm and let them steam for 10 minutes. Peel off the blackened skins and discard. Cut out the stems and seeds and discard, then cut the peppers into fine strips.

Cut the broccoli into bite-sized florets. Bring a large saucepan of water to the boil and add the broccoli. Cook for 1 minute, then drain and refresh under cold water. Put in iced water to stop the cooking process.

Heat a frying pan until hot and toast the pine nuts, tossing them in the pan frequently, until browned. Set aside. Cook the bacon in the pan and cut it into thin strips. Set aside until needed.

Drain the broccoli and put it in a bowl with the peppers, pine nuts, bacon and chillies.

Heat the olive oil over medium heat (in the same frying pan). Add the breadcrumbs and garlic and cook, tossing them around the pan, for 2–3 minutes until golden. Set aside to cool.

To make the caper and anchovy dressing, combine the sugar, capers and anchovies in a small bowl. Season to taste with salt and pepper, then whisk in the lemon juice, vinegar and, finally, the extra virgin olive oil.

Pour the dressing over the salad and mix well. Just before serving, top with the breadcrumbs and garlic.

The perfect accompaniment to barbecues, potato salad is essential summer fare. This version makes a change from the usual, looks stunning and is packed with flavour, making it great for those bring-a-plate occasions. If time is short, you can use good-quality bought mayonnaise combined with a squeeze of lemon juice.

new potato, crisp salami and sesame salad

800 g waxy new potatoes

a pinch of sea salt

2 tablespoons sesame seeds

150 g thinly sliced salami (a fatty, unflavoured variety)

½ quantity lemon mayonnaise (see below)

75 g rocket

a small bunch of dill, chopped

lemon mayonnaise

1 egg yolk, at room temperature

2 tablespoons freshly squeezed lemon juice

a pinch of sea salt

125 ml plain-flavoured oil, such as grape seed

1 teaspoon sesame oil

SERVES 6

To make the lemon mayonnaise, put the egg yolk, half the lemon juice and salt in a bowl or the plastic beaker of a hand-held blender. Whisk to mix. While whisking continuously, slowly add the plain-flavoured oil a drop at a time until fully incorporated. Whisk in the sesame oil and remaining lemon juice. Cover and set aside until needed. (Note that this recipe makes approximately double the quantity required for this salad. The remainder will keep in the refrigerator for up to 3 days.)

If necessary, cut the potatoes into even-sized pieces. Put in a large saucepan. Cover with cold water, add the salt, bring to the boil, then simmer until tender. Drain and set aside.

Heat a frying pan to medium heat, add the sesame seeds and toast for about 6–8 minutes, stirring until golden. Set aside.

Reheat the frying pan until hot, add the salami slices and cook for a few minutes on each side until browned. Remove and drain on kitchen paper. (It will crisp up more as it cools.)

Arrange the rocket in a serving bowl. Toss the potatoes with the lemon mayonnaise and pile on top of the rocket. Scatter with half the toasted sesame seeds and dill. Crumble over the crisp salami and scatter with the remaining sesame seeds and dill to serve.

For a delicious side to serve at a barbecue or for a light summer lunch, look no further than fattoush, a traditional Middle Eastern salad that showcases the juicy ripeness of the tomato harvest. Roasting tomatoes condenses their flavour, but if you are lucky enough to have particularly tasty tomatoes, do leave them raw.

roasted tomato and red pepper fattoush

8 tomatoes

2 red peppers, halved and deseeded

6 tablespoons olive oil

3 tablespoons oregano or marjoram leaves

2 large pita breads

1 small red onion, sliced

½ cucumber, chopped

a large bunch of flat leaf parsley, roughly chopped

a small bunch of mint, roughly chopped

freshly squeezed juice of 1 lemon

sea salt and freshly ground black pepper

SERVES 6

Preheat the oven to 150°C (300°F) Gas 2.

Cut the tomatoes in half and scoop out the seeds. Put the deseeded tomatoes and red peppers cut-side up on a baking tray. Drizzle with 2 tablespoons of the oil, add a little salt and pepper and sprinkle the oregano leaves over the top. Bake in the preheated oven for 1 hour. Let cool and then slice the roasted peppers into strips.

Raise the oven temperature to 200°C (400°F) Gas 6.

Carefully split the pita breads in half through the middle and place rough-side up on a baking tray. Bake for 10 minutes until crisp. Let cool on a wire rack.

In a serving bowl, combine the roasted peppers and tomatoes, onion, cucumber, parsley and mint. Toss through the lemon juice and 2 tablespoons of the oil and season with salt and pepper. Break the baked pita breads into pieces and scatter these over the salad. Drizzle with the remaining oil to serve.

iceberg, blue cheese and date salad with saffron and walnut dressing

1 iceberg lettuce

200 g creamy blue cheese

8 dried medjool dates

70 g walnuts

a large handful of micro greens (sprouts)*

saffron and walnut dressing

½ teaspoon saffron threads

2 tablespoons freshly squeezed orange juice

1 tablespoon white wine vinegar

½ teaspoon sea salt

6 tablespoons walnut oil

SERVES 6

see glossary pages 140–141

This salad is all about texture and taste with the added bonus of being simple to prepare and looking stunning. Micro greens look great and have a delicate sweet flavour, but alfalfa or broccoli sprouts are also good.

To make the saffron and walnut dressing, put the saffron and orange juice in a bowl and leave to infuse for about 10 minutes. Whisk in the vinegar and salt, then the oil, whisking continuously. Cover and set aside until needed.

Slice the lettuce into 8 wedges, then cut each wedge into 3 pieces, giving you a total of 24 pieces. Arrange them in a serving bowl.

Cut the cheese into 12 pieces and arrange these among the lettuce. Chop the dates into 4 and discard the stones. Scatter them over the lettuce along with the walnuts. Pour over the dressing, then scatter over the micro greens. Serve immediately.

Roast vegetable salads are flavoursome and hearty, and go with just about everything. The cucumber-scented dressing adds a freshness and is also terrific drizzled over vegetable kebabs.

cumin-roasted vegetables
with cucumber-scented yoghurt dressing

6 medium or 18 small carrots, scrubbed or peeled

2 tablespoons olive oil

6 courgettes

12 small tomatoes

2 teaspoons cumin seeds

1 teaspoon sea salt flakes

420-g tin chickpeas, drained

leaves from a large bunch of basil

leaves from a small bunch of marjoram or mint

½ teaspoon ground sumac*

extra virgin olive oil, for drizzling

cucumber-scented yoghurt dressing

⅛ cucumber, roughly chopped

2 tablespoons freshly squeezed lemon juice

½ teaspoon sea salt

3 tablespoons tahini*

200 ml natural yoghurt

SERVES 6

see glossary pages 140–141

Preheat the oven to 220°C (425°F) Gas 7.

Cut the carrots in half crossways, then into quarters, lengthways or in half lengthways if small. Toss with 1 tablespoon of the olive oil. Arrange in a roasting tray and roast in the preheated oven for 10 minutes.

Cut the courgettes in half crossways, then into quarters lengthways. Put in a bowl with the tomatoes and toss with the remaining olive oil, cumin seeds and salt. Remove the carrots from the oven and add the courgettes and tomatoes. Stir together to coat everything with cumin. Return the tray to the oven and roast for a further 10 minutes. Let cool.

To make the cucumber-scented yoghurt dressing, put the cucumber, lemon juice and salt in a blender or food processor. Blend to a pulp (you will need to shake down the cucumber a few times). Put in a nylon sieve over a bowl and let drain for about 15 minutes. Discard the pulp. In a bowl, whisk together the cucumber juice and tahini, then whisk in the yoghurt.

Put the chickpeas in a bowl and, using a potato masher or fork, lightly crush them. Arrange the roast vegetables around the outside of a serving plate, top with the crushed chickpeas and scatter the basil and marjoram over the top. Pour the dressing into the centre of the plate and drizzle with extra virgin olive oil. Sprinkle with sumac and serve immediately.

This is a more dramatic take on the old-style bean salad and is the perfect foil to rich meats such as sausages. The lemon and poppy seed dressing works well with any green salad or potato salad and is delicious drizzled over grilled courgettes and aubergine.

five-bean salad with lemon and poppy seed dressing

420-g tin white beans (butter or cannellini), drained and rinsed

420-g tin borlotti beans, drained and rinsed

300 g green beans, trimmed

75 g small fresh or 150 g frozen broad beans

120 g beansprouts

lemon and poppy seed dressing

3 tablespoons poppy seeds

1 small red onion

1 tablespoon runny honey

1 teaspoon finely grated lemon zest

1 teaspoon sea salt flakes

¼ teaspoon freshly ground black pepper

2 tablespoons freshly squeezed lemon juice

4 tablespoons olive oil, lemon-infused if available

SERVES 6

To make the lemon and poppy seed dressing, heat a frying pan over medium heat and add the poppy seeds. Cook, tossing in the pan, for 3 minutes until toasted. Let cool.

Grate the onion and put in a bowl with the toasted poppy seeds, honey, lemon zest, salt and pepper. Whisk in the lemon juice and then the oil.

In a large bowl, combine the drained cannellini and borlotti beans. Pour over the lemon and poppy seed dressing and toss well. Set aside while you prepare the other beans.

Bring a saucepan of water to the boil. Add the green beans and boil for 5 minutes until just tender. Drain and refresh in plenty of iced water.

Bring another saucepan of water to the boil. Add the broad beans and boil for 2 minutes until just blanched. Drain and refresh in plenty of iced water. If using frozen beans, peel off the tough outer layer and discard.

Pour a jug of boiling water over the beansprouts to blanch, then refresh in plenty of iced water.

Drain the green beans, broad beans and beansprouts well. Add to the dressed beans and toss well before serving.

brown rice, hazelnut and herb salad with kaffir lime dressing

½ teaspoon sea salt

200 g brown rice

140 g hazelnuts

4 spring onions, thinly sliced

leaves from a large bunch of mint

leaves from a large bunch of basil, Thai basil if available

leaves from a large bunch of coriander

2 teaspoons sesame oil

edible flower petals (optional)

kaffir lime dressing

1 tablespoon sugar, preferably palm*, chopped

2 tablespoons rice vinegar*

1 tablespoon Japanese* or golden soy sauce*

1 tablespoon freshly squeezed lime juice

1 tablespoon Thai fish sauce*

2 kaffir lime leaves*, tough stems removed, very finely shredded

SERVES 6

*see glossary pages 140–141

Rice salads are a perennial favourite at barbecues and buffets. This deliciously nutty version has a hint of South-east Asian flavour. Great with fish and shellfish, it's also good with meats that have been cooked on the barbecue, especially ones that have been marinated in soy sauce. Cook the rice the day you are making the salad, as it will go hard if refrigerated for too long.

To make the kaffir lime dressing, gently heat the sugar and vinegar together in a small saucepan, stirring until the sugar has dissolved. Let cool, then combine with the soy sauce, lime juice, fish sauce and kaffir lime leaves. Set aside until needed.

Bring 500 ml water to the boil, add the salt and rice and bring back to the boil. Stir, cover, lower the heat to very low and cook undisturbed for 25 minutes. Turn off the heat, let rest for 5 minutes, then stir with a fork to fluff up (drain off excess water if necessary). Put in a serving bowl, toss with the dressing and leave to cool.

Preheat the oven to 170°C (325°F) Gas 3.

Spread the hazelnuts out on a baking tray. Toast in the preheated oven for 12 minutes, stirring once. Put the nuts in a clean tea towel and rub vigorously until the skins come loose. Shake or blow the loosened skins away, and continue rubbing the nuts until they are mostly free from skins. Roughly chop.

Toss the rice with the hazelnuts, spring onions, mint, basil, coriander and oil. Scatter with edible petals, if using, to serve.

warm sides

Simple roast potatoes are endlessly popular, but sometimes it's fun to jazz them up with extra flavour. For really crisp roast potatoes, I prefer to pre-boil them to ensure that crunchy, roughed-up edge.

roast garlic potatoes with chorizo, lemon slices and rosemary

1 kg floury potatoes

3 whole garlic bulbs

3 tablespoons olive oil or duck or goose fat

3 chorizo sausages, diagonally sliced

1 lemon, halved lengthways and sliced

2 tablespoons rosemary needles

sea salt flakes

SERVES 6

Preheat the oven to 200°C (400°F) Gas 6.

Cut the potatoes into large pieces. Put in a large saucepan and cover with water. Bring to the boil and boil for 5 minutes. Drain in a colander or sieve and leave to steam/dry out for 5 minutes. Toss the potatoes around in the sieve or colander to rough up the outsides.

Cut the garlic bulbs in half crossways.

Pour the oil into a large roasting tray. Put in the preheated oven for 5 minutes to heat. Add the potatoes and garlic to the hot oil with plenty of salt flakes and stir well to coat.

Roast for a total of 40 minutes, but remove the tray from the oven after 20 minutes, stir well and add the chorizo, lemon and rosemary. Return the tray to the hot oven and continue roasting for a further 20 minutes. Serve immediately.

portuguese potatoes

4 tablespoons olive oil

1.5 kg small waxy new potatoes

6 garlic cloves

3 sprigs of rosemary

2 teaspoons sea salt flakes

SERVES 6

This is the perfect cooking method for small waxy potatoes. I have adapted it from the delicious pot-roasted potatoes I enjoyed in Coimbra, Portugal. I cook these non-stop in spring, as that's when our potatoes in New Zealand are tiny and abundant.

Heat the oil in a large, heavy-based, flame-proof casserole set over medium heat. Add the potatoes. Using your knife, crush the garlic cloves, discard the skins and add the garlic to the oil and potatoes along with the rosemary and salt. Stir well, reduce the heat to low, then cover and cook for 50–60 minutes for walnut-sized potatoes or 1–1¼ hours for egg-sized ones, stirring occasionally.

NOTE These Portuguese-style potatoes are also delicious as a cold side dish. You can make them the day before, and once cool, cover and refrigerate. Bring back to room temperature for 1 hour before serving.

crushed peas

2 tablespoons olive oil

1 onion, thinly sliced

4 sage leaves

a small bunch of celery tops

625 g frozen peas

60 ml single cream

sea salt and freshly ground black pepper

kitchen string

SERVES 6

Peas are always a great stand-by side dish because almost everyone already has a bag in the freezer! They also have the added bonus of being delicious and making a good accompaniment to most foods.

Heat the oil in a saucepan over medium heat. Add the onion and cook gently for 5 minutes, stirring frequently.

Tie together the sage leaves and celery tops with a piece of kitchen string (for easy removal) and add to the onion along with the peas. Stir, cover and cook for 10 minutes, stirring occasionally.

Uncover, stir through the cream and heat through. Take off the heat and, using a potato masher, gently mash the peas. Season to taste with salt and pepper and serve immediately.

This summery, dairy-free version of the Swedish classic, Janssen's Temptation, tastes amazing as an accompaniment to lamb, fish or chicken. If you are using mild-tasting anchovies, use 110 g; if you are using the stronger-flavoured varieties use 50 g.

mediterranean temptation

3 tablespoons olive oil

2 large onions, thinly sliced

4 medium–large, all-purpose, or waxy potatoes, peeled

50 g–110 g anchovy fillets (see recipe introduction)

80 g black olives, stoned

4 tablespoons drained capers

¼ teaspoon white pepper

300 ml vegetable stock

15 g fresh white breadcrumbs

a 28 x 20-cm baking dish

SERVES 6

Preheat the oven to 180°C (350°F) Gas 4. Brush a baking dish with a little oil.

Heat 2 tablespoons of the oil in a large frying pan set over low/medium heat, add the onions and cook, stirring occasionally, for 20 minutes until soft but not brown.

Coarsely grate the potatoes. (Use a mandoline if you have one to get long, fine julienne.) Mix the potatoes with the onions, anchovies, olives and capers, and season with the pepper.

Spoon the mixture into the prepared baking dish. In a saucepan, heat the stock until hot and pour it over the dish. Top with the breadcrumbs and drizzle with the remaining oil.

Bake in the preheated oven for about 1 hour or until golden and bubbling. Serve warm.

375 ml vegetable stock

175 g couscous

2 garlic cloves, crushed

finely grated zest of 2 lemons

4 tablespoons olive oil

2 red peppers, deseeded and
thickly sliced

3 courgettes, sliced lengthways
and then diagonally across

1 aubergine, cut into
slices 1 cm thick

1 red onion, cut into wedges

150 g almonds, toasted

sea salt and freshly ground
black pepper

herb dressing

3 tablespoons cider vinegar

a small bunch of flat leaf
parsley, chopped

a small bunch of mint, chopped

2 tablespoons chopped oregano

2 tablespoons chopped chives

6 tablespoons olive oil

sea salt and freshly ground
black pepper

SERVES 6

grilled vegetable and almond
couscous with herb dressing

Couscous is an ideal solution for those preparing a meal in a hurry,
as it's incredibly fast and simple. Here the couscous is mixed with
grilled veggies and given a flavour boost with a herbed dressing.

To make the herb dressing, whisk together the vinegar and oil in a small
bowl and add all the herbs. Mix well to combine and season to taste with
salt and pepper. Set aside until needed.

Bring the stock to the boil in a large saucepan, then stir in the couscous.
Remove from the heat, cover and leave to absorb for 10 minutes. Season
to taste with salt and pepper and then fluff up well with a fork.

Meanwhile, combine the garlic and lemon zest with 2 tablespoons of
the oil in a small bowl and season to taste with salt and pepper.

Heat a griddle pan to hot. Put the peppers, courgettes, aubergine and
onion in a bowl with the remaining 2 tablespoons oil and toss to coat.
Cook the vegetables in the griddle pan for 3 minutes on each side until
tender. Cut the cooked aubergine slices into quarters and place in
a large bowl with the other vegetables. Add the couscous and almonds
and toss to combine.

Spoon the mixture onto a warmed serving platter and spoon over the
herbed dressing to serve.

wok-fried aubergine and courgette with spicy sauce

4 Japanese aubergines*

4 courgettes

1 tablespoon groundnut oil

3 garlic cloves, finely chopped

60 ml fish, chicken or
vegetable stock

spicy sauce

3 tablespoons Japanese
mayonnaise* or other
good-quality mayonnaise

1 tablespoon mild soy sauce

1 teaspoon rice vinegar*

1 teaspoon mirin*(optional)

½ teaspoon Japanese
seven-spice powder*
or crushed dried red chilli flakes

½ teaspoon sesame oil

SERVES 4–6

*see glossary pages 140–141

This tasty Japanese-style dish uses the roll-cutting method for the vegetables to give a greater cut surface area that allows more even cooking.

To make the spicy sauce, combine the mayonnaise, soy sauce, vinegar, mirin, seven-spice powder and sesame oil in a bowl and set aside.

Trim the ends off the aubergines and courgettes and roll-cut into 3–4 cm pieces. To do this, put the vegetables on a chopping board horizontally. Make a cut on the diagonal at one end, roll the aubergine 180°, then make another diagonal cut at the same angle to give a triangular piece.

Heat the groundnut oil in a wok or large frying pan over high heat, add the aubergines, courgettes and garlic and stir-fry for 2 minutes. Add the stock and cook, stirring, for a further 4 minutes.

Transfer the vegetables to a serving dish and pour over the spicy sauce. Serve immediately.

roasted sweet potato and macadamia nut salad

3 sweet potatoes
(about 300 g each), peeled

1 tablespoon olive oil

1 teaspoon sea salt flakes

70 g raw macadamia nuts,
roughly chopped

200 g baby spinach leaves,
washed

dressing

1 tablespoon cider vinegar

1 teaspoon wholegrain mustard

2 tablespoons macadamia
or olive oil

sea salt and freshly ground
black pepper

SERVES 4

Macadamia nuts add a great crunch to this salad, but can be replaced by any other nuts or even toasted sunflower or pumpkin seeds if you prefer.

Preheat the oven to 190°C (375°F) Gas 5.

Cut the sweet potatoes into cubes 2 cm in size and toss in a bowl with the olive oil and salt flakes. Tip onto a baking tray and roast in the preheated oven for 10 minutes.

Put the macadamia nuts in the bowl and toss with any residual oil. Add to the sweet potatoes and roast in the hot oven for 10 minutes, giving the sweet potatoes 20 minutes in total.

To make the dressing, mix together the vinegar, mustard and macadamia oil in a small bowl. Season to taste with salt and pepper.

Arrange the spinach leaves on a serving platter and top with the sweet potatoes and macadamia nuts. Drizzle or spoon the dressing over the top and serve immediately.

3 tablespoons olive oil

1 onion, sliced

3 garlic cloves, crushed

a small bunch of flat leaf parsley, chopped

1 large aubergine, chopped

2–3 red and/or yellow peppers, deseeded and chopped

4 courgettes, sliced

¼ teaspoon sea salt

4 large tomatoes, skinned and chopped, OR a 400-g tin peeled plum tomatoes

2 teaspoons red wine vinegar or balsamic vinegar (optional)

sea salt and freshly ground black pepper

SERVES 6

My personal favourite, ratatouille is simply the best all-purpose summer side there is. Best made when courgettes, aubergines and tomatoes are in season, it goes perfectly with any main course or serve with rice or couscous for a vegetarian meal.

ratatouille

Heat the oil in a large, heavy-based saucepan set over medium heat. Add the onion, garlic and parsley and sauté for 10 minutes, stirring regularly.

Add the aubergine and cook for 5 minutes. Add the peppers and courgettes and stir in the salt. Cook for a few minutes, then add the chopped tomatoes.

Cover and cook for 5 minutes until the tomatoes start to break down, then uncover and cook for 10–15 minutes until the vegetables are tender, adding a little water if necessary. Season to taste with vinegar, if using, and salt and pepper. Serve warm.

Pumpkin works wonderfully well in this fragrant dish, but it's also delicious made with butternut squash or sweet potato. Fresh curry leaves make all the difference, so do try and find them if you can.

coconut-roasted pumpkin with cashew and coriander crumble

70 g cashew nuts

1 tablespoon palm sugar* or brown sugar

½ teaspoon turmeric

3 cm piece of fresh ginger, peeled and grated OR ¼ teaspoon ground ginger

½ teaspoon sea salt

100 ml coconut cream

1.2 kg pumpkin, peeled, deseeded and sliced

leaves from 4 stems of curry leaves* (optional)

50 g shredded coconut

a small bunch of coriander, chopped

SERVES 6

*see glossary pages 140–141

Preheat the oven to 190°C (375°F) Gas 5.

Spread the cashew nuts out on a baking tray and toast in the preheated oven for 10 minutes. Let cool.

Chop the palm sugar finely, if using. In a large bowl, mix together the sugar, turmeric, ginger and salt, then stir in the coconut cream. Add the prepared pumpkin and toss with the coconut cream mixture.

Spread the pumpkin out on a baking tray lined with baking parchment. Cook in the hot oven for 20 minutes, stirring once. Remove from the oven and add the curry leaves, if using, and shredded coconut. Toss to combine and cook for a further 5 minutes.

Finely chop the cooled cashew nuts and combine with the coriander. Arrange the pumpkin on a serving dish and scatter over the cashew and coriander crumble mixture.

2 tablespoons butter

1 tablespoon olive oil

2 onions, cut into wedges

250 g yams, peeled
and chopped

250 g sweet potatoes, peeled
and cut into large chunks

250 g baby carrots, scrubbed
or peeled if necessary

250 g parsnips, peeled and cut
into large chunks

1 tablespoon runny honey

2 tablespoons grated fresh
ginger

1 cinnamon stick, broken in half

100 g stoned prunes

500 ml vegetable stock

sea salt and freshly ground
black pepper to taste

SERVES 6

tagine of root vegetables

Serve this fragrant Moroccan-style vegetable tagine with bread to soak up the tasty juices. It is a warming accompaniment to roast or barbecued chicken or lamb, or can be served on its own as a vegetarian meal with rice or buttery couscous.

Preheat the oven to 180°C (350°F) Gas 4.

Heat the butter and oil in a tagine or flame-proof lidded casserole. Add the onions and cook for 5 minutes until softened.

Add the yams, sweet potatoes, carrots and parsnips and cook, stirring occasionally, for 5 minutes. Add the honey, ginger, cinnamon and prunes and season to taste with salt and pepper. Pour in the stock.

Cover and bake in the preheated oven for 45 minutes, uncovering for the final 15 minutes of cooking. Serve warm.

brussels sprouts, lettuce and cabbage sauté

400 g Brussels sprouts

1 tablespoon olive oil

1 tablespoon butter

1 teaspoon caraway seeds

¼ green cabbage, thinly sliced

½ iceberg lettuce, cut into 1-cm slices

freshly squeezed juice of ½ lemon

½ teaspoon sea salt

SERVES 4–6

This method of cooking sprouts and cabbage ensures that they remain crisp and tasty. A great match with duck, goose or pork.

Separate as many leaves as you can from the sprouts and then finely slice any remaining leaves that are too tight to separate. Set aside.

Heat a large sauté pan or wok. Add the oil and butter and heat to medium. Add the caraway seeds and sizzle for about 30 seconds. Add the Brussels sprouts and cabbage and stir-fry for about 4 minutes until wilted. Add the lettuce, stir-fry for a further minute, then quickly transfer to a serving dish to stop the cooking. Pour over the lemon juice and sprinkle with the salt. Toss and serve immediately.

three-nut pilaf

2 tablespoons olive oil

70 g blanched almonds, roughly chopped

70 g pistachio nuts, roughly chopped

70 g pine nuts

½ teaspoon saffron threads

2 tablespoons butter

1 onion, finely chopped

1 cinnamon stick

300 g basmati rice

750 ml chicken stock, boiling

leaves from a small bunch of parsley, coriander or mint, chopped

SERVES 6

For a chewier result, you can use brown basmati rice and increase the cooking time to 25 minutes. Though this recipe has a warm, spicy feel about it, it goes well with most foods.

Heat 1 tablespoon of the oil in a heavy-based saucepan set over medium heat. Add the almonds, pistachios and pine nuts and cook for 5 minutes until brown. Set aside.

Put the saffron threads in a small bowl with a little warm water and leave to soak.

Heat the remaining oil and butter in the saucepan and add the onion and cinnamon. Cook for 5 minutes, then stir in the rice and cook for a further 3 minutes, stirring continuously. Add the stock, and bring to the boil. Reduce to a very low simmer, cover and cook for 15 minutes without disturbing. Remove from the heat. Uncover and pour over the soaked saffron. Cover immediately and let rest, covered, for 5 minutes.

Reserve a few nuts and some herbs for garnish. Stir the remaining nuts and herbs through the rice. Sprinkle over the garnish and serve warm.

sun-dried tomato and sweetcorn bread

2 tablespoons olive oil

175 g coarse yellow cornmeal or instant polenta

125 g plain flour

1 teaspoon baking powder

1 tablespoon rosemary needles

½ teaspoon sea salt

1 egg

250 ml buttermilk

250 ml milk

150 g sweetcorn kernels, fresh or tinned

80 g sun-dried tomatoes, chopped

a heavy baking dish, 28 cm diameter, preferably cast-iron

SERVES 6

Cornbread is a wonderfully easy bread to make at home, so great to whip up when you want fresh bread, hot from the oven. It is best made in a heavy, cast-iron cooking dish, a skillet or a cast-iron frying pan to achieve a crisp outer crust.

Preheat the oven to 200°C (400°F) Gas 6.

Coat the bottom and sides of the baking dish with the oil. Put in the preheated oven to heat up for 5 minutes.

Combine the cornmeal, flour, baking powder, rosemary and salt in a bowl. Beat together the egg, buttermilk and milk, then carefully fold it into the flour mixture along with the sweetcorn and sun-dried tomatoes.

Remove the baking dish from the oven and pour in the batter. Bake for 30 minutes until set and golden. Let cool on a wire rack.

Slice into wedges to serve. The bread is best eaten while still warm.

garlic and tomato naan

2 tomatoes

50 g butter, softened

2 garlic cloves, crushed

2 tablespoons oregano leaves, chopped

2 x 125-g naan breads

sea salt and freshly ground black pepper

SERVES 4-6

This recipe calls for puffy naan bread. If none is available, you can use an Italian ciabatta loaf. Slice it in half through the middle and spread the butter over the cut sides.

Preheat the oven to 200°C (400°F) Gas 6.

Cut a small cross in the base of each tomato and put in a saucepan. Pour over boiling water to cover. Leave for 1 minute, remove and peel off the skins. Cut the tomatoes into quarters and remove and discard the seeds. Finely chop the flesh. Let cool.

Put the softened butter, garlic and oregano in a bowl and mix well. Add the chopped tomatoes and mix well to combine. Spread each naan bread with half of the mixture. Season to taste with salt and pepper.

Bake in the preheated oven for 10–15 minutes until hot. Cut into slices and serve immediately.

olive oil and garlic bread

1 baguette (French stick)

4 tablespoons olive oil

4 garlic cloves, crushed

½ teaspoon sea salt flakes

SERVES 6–8

This is a dairy-free version of the favourite bread. I use sea salt flakes such as Maldon, as they add texture. If none are available, reduce the quantity of salt to ¼ teaspoon.

Preheat the oven to 200°C (400°F) Gas 6.

Slice the baguette on the diagonal at 3 cm intervals, being careful not to cut all the way through the base. Put on a long piece of foil.

In a small bowl, combine the oil, garlic and salt. Using a spoon, drizzle a little of the oil between each slice of baguette, then brush the remaining oil over the top. Wrap in the foil.

Bake in the preheated oven for 10 minutes until hot through. Serve the bread immediately.

poppy seed and garlic bagel toasts

3 plain bagels

3 tablespoons olive oil

2 garlic cloves, crushed

1 tablespoon poppy seeds

SERVES 4

There is no comparison between shop-bought and home-made bagel toasts. They are also dead simple to make. Try them with dips or serve as part of a buffet bread basket.

Preheat the grill to hot.

Slice each bagel into 4 and arrange on the grill pan. Grill one side until browned. Remove from the grill and turn over.

Combine the oil and garlic in a bowl and brush over the untoasted side of the bagels. Scatter over the poppy seeds and return to the grill. Toast until crisp and golden.

Serve immediately or let cool and store in an airtight container for up to 2 days.

main course salads

Roasting beetroot takes time, but it is worth it for the resulting wonderfully sweet flavour. If you have a barbecue going, try wrapping the beetroot in foil and baking them in the embers. The feta can be replaced with grilled halloumi if preferred.

roast beetroot, orange and feta salad

600 g baby or small beetroot, unpeeled and trimmed

1 red onion

a large handful of crisp salad leaves

3 oranges

150 g walnuts or hazelnuts

200 g feta cheese, cubed

a small bunch of flat leaf parsley, roughly chopped

micro greens (sprouts)*, to garnish (optional)

honey cider vinaigrette

1 tablespoon runny honey

½ teaspoon sea salt

¼ teaspoon white pepper

2 tablespoons cider vinegar

4 tablespoons olive oil

SERVES 4

*see glossary pages 140–141

Preheat the oven to 180°C (350°F) Gas 4.

To make the honey cider vinaigette, combine the honey, salt, pepper and vinegar in a small bowl and whisk in the oil. Set aside.

Put the unpeeled beetroot on a baking tray and bake in the preheated oven until tender – about 30 minutes for baby beets, 45 minutes for small beets. Remove from the oven and let cool. When cool enough to handle, peel off the skins – they should come away easily in your fingers. Trim the ends and discard. Cut the beetroot in half if necessary and toss with a little of the honey cider vinaigrette. Set aside.

Slice the onion very finely, using a mandoline if you have one. Put in a bowl of iced water for 10 minutes. Drain well.

Put the salad leaves on a serving platter. With a sharp knife, remove the rind and all the white pith from the oranges. Slice and arrange on top of the salad leaves.

Heat a frying pan, add the walnuts and toast for a couple of minutes until browned. Scatter these over the leaves and oranges with the beetroot and onion. Drizzle over the honey cider vinaigrette. Scatter the feta over the salad and sprinkle with the parsley and micro greens, if using. Serve immediately.

This recipe is true to the original classic Caesar salad – a rare perfection. Adding any of the variations listed below will turn this into a more substantial meal.

classic caesar salad

2 thick slices of dense white bread

2 tablespoons olive oil

1 large or 3 baby cos lettuce

40 g Parmesan cheese, grated or shaved

classic caesar dressing

1 very fresh egg, at room temperature

1 small garlic clove, crushed

1 teaspoon Dijon mustard

1 teaspoon Worcestershire sauce

¼ teaspoon sea salt

⅛ teaspoon freshly ground black pepper

1 tablespoon white wine vinegar

1 tablespoon freshly squeezed lemon juice

4 tablespoons extra virgin olive oil

SERVES 4

Cut the crusts off the bread and discard. Cut the bread into cubes. Heat the olive oil in a frying pan, add the bread cubes and cook until golden brown. Set aside.

To make the classic Caesar dressing, put the egg in a small saucepan and cover with warm water. Bring to just simmering, turn off the heat and leave the egg for 2 minutes. Run under cold water to stop the egg cooking further.

Crack the egg into a large serving bowl and whisk in the garlic, mustard, Worcestershire sauce, salt, pepper, vinegar and lemon juice. Slowly whisk in the extra virgin olive oil.

Add the lettuce and toss well, then scatter over the Parmesan cheese and croûtons to serve.

Variations:

Chicken Caesar Roast 3–4 chicken breasts, preferably in a roasting bag to prevent them drying out, until golden and cooked through. Let cool then slice and add to the salad.

Bacon and avocado Caesar Fry 8 rashers of bacon until crisp. Chop and add to the salad with 1 sliced avocado.

Poached egg and anchovy Caesar For a more intense anchovy flavour, you can either add 4 finely chopped anchovy fillets to the dressing or toss whole, mild, good-quality anchovy fillets or marinated anchovies through the salad. Top each salad with a poached egg to serve.

NOTE This recipe uses partially cooked eggs. If you prefer to cook the eggs through, you can do this by increasing the cooking time to 6 minutes. Finely chop the egg before adding it to the dressing.

greek barley salad

This hearty version of the traditional and much-loved salad incorporates satisfyingly chewy barley. If you are able to buy good-quality dried Greek oregano from speciality food stores, it will make all the difference to the flavour.

100 g pearl barley

freshly squeezed juice and finely grated zest of 1 lemon

2 teaspoons white or red wine vinegar

4 tablespoons extra virgin olive oil

1 red onion, thinly sliced

4 tomatoes, chopped

1 large cucumber or 2 small (Lebanese), deseeded and chopped

1 green pepper, deseeded and chopped

20 kalamata olives

150 g feta cheese

1 teaspoon dried oregano

sea salt and freshly ground black pepper

SERVES 4

Cook the barley in a saucepan of boiling salted water for 30 minutes or until tender. Drain and set aside until needed.

In a large serving bowl, whisk together the lemon juice and zest, vinegar and oil, then stir in the warm barley and mix well. Let cool.

Soak the onion in a bowl of iced water for 10 minutes. Drain well.

Add the drained onion to the barley along with the tomatoes, cucumber, green pepper and olives and mix to combine. Season to taste with salt and pepper.

Crumble the feta over the top of the salad and sprinkle with oregano. Serve immediately.

tuna and cannellini bean salad

1 red onion, thinly sliced

185-g tin or jar tuna in olive oil, drained

410-g tin cannellini beans, drained and rinsed

a large bunch of flat leaf parsley, chopped

freshly squeezed juice of 1 lemon

4 tablespoons extra virgin olive oil

sea salt and freshly ground black pepper

fresh bread, to serve

SERVES 2–3

This uncomplicated salad was taught to me by my Italian neighbour, Lucio Di Nora, a fantastic cook. Served with fresh bread it is a filling meal, and as it features two tinned ingredients you can usually whip it up at short notice. If you have tuna in good-quality olive oil, use the oil in the salad.

Soak the onion slices in iced water for 10 minutes. Drain well.

Put the onion, tuna, cannellini beans and parsley in a large serving bowl. Add the lemon juice and oil and toss gently to combine.

Season to taste with salt and pepper. Serve with plenty of fresh bread.

Inspired by the wonderful Two Fat Ladies, this salad is really just a smart version of a mixed grill. If you have young, tender broad beans, there is no need to peel them.

bacon, egg and bean salad
with grilled chorizo on toast

250 g fresh or 500 g frozen broad beans

200 g rashers of streaky bacon

6 eggs, at room temperature

3 tablespoons freshly squeezed lemon juice

½ teaspoon sugar

¼ teaspoon sea salt

freshly ground black pepper

6 tablespoons extra virgin olive oil

6 chorizo sausages

200 g baby spinach leaves, washed

6 slices of crusty bread, such as ciabatta, toasted

SERVES 6

Bring a saucepan of water to the boil and add the broad beans. Return the water to the boil, then cook the beans for 2 minutes until tender. Drain, refresh in iced water to cool and peel if necessary.

Heat a frying pan, add the bacon and cook until crisp. Cut into pieces and set aside.

Fill a saucepan with water, add the eggs and place over a medum/high heat. Bring to the boil and then continue to boil for 2 minutes (6 minutes if you would like hard-boiled eggs). Drain and refresh with cold water. When cool enough to handle, peel and set aside.

In a large bowl, whisk together the lemon juice, sugar, salt, pepper and oil and set aside. Add the spinach and toss to coat. Set aside.

Preheat the grill to hot. Cut the chorizo into slices and put under the hot grill for 5 minutes, turning once, until heated through.

To serve, arrange the dressed spinach, broad beans and bacon on plates. Cut the eggs into halves or quarters and place on the plates. Top each piece of toast with the chorizo slices and serve with the salad.

lemon-rubbed lamb and orzo salad

This colourful salad can be made well ahead of time; just cook and add the lamb before serving. It's full of the flavours of summer.

3 garlic cloves, crushed

finely grated zest of 2 lemons and freshly squeezed juice of 1

3 tablespoons olive oil

300-g piece of lean lamb fillet

1 large red pepper

1 large yellow pepper

250 g orzo pasta*

20 cherry tomatoes

400-g tin or jar artichoke hearts, drained and quartered

a small red onion, thinly sliced

4 tablespoons fresh or bottled pesto

4 tablespoons pine nuts, toasted

leaves from a small bunch of basil

sea salt and freshly ground black pepper

SERVES 4

see glossary pages 140–141

Preheat the oven to 220°C (425°F) Gas 7.

In a small bowl, combine the garlic and lemon zest with 1 tablespoon of the oil and season with salt and pepper. Rub this over the lamb and set aside until needed.

Preheat the grill to hot. Put the lamb under the grill and cook for 2 minutes each side, then transfer to a roasting tray and cook in the preheated oven for 5 minutes for medium rare or up to 10 minutes for more well done. Remove from the oven, wrap in foil and leave to rest for 10 minutes.

Cut the peppers into thick strips, discarding the stems and seeds. Cook under the hot grill until tender. Set aside.

Cook the orzo according to the packet instructions. Drain and toss with the remaining 2 tablespoons oil, lemon juice, peppers, cherry tomatoes, artichokes, onion and pesto.

Place the salad on a serving platter. Slice the lamb and arrange it on top. Scatter with the pine nuts and basil leaves to serve.

pickled salmon with fennel and cucumber salad

500-g salmon fillet, skinned and boned

3–4 shallots, thinly sliced

4 tablespoons chopped dill

1 fennel bulb, with fronds if possible

½ cucumber, halved lengthways and deseeded

freshly squeezed juice of 1 lemon

1 teaspoon wholegrain mustard

3 tablespoons olive oil, plus extra for drizzling (optional)

sea salt and freshly ground black pepper

pickling liquid

200 ml white or rice vinegar*

2 teaspoons sea salt

4 tablespoons sugar

finely grated zest of 1 lemon

SERVES 4

see glossary pages 140–141

Serve this spring salad with new potatoes to make a complete meal. The fish is marinated for several days, so do prepare ahead.

To make the pickling liquid, combine the vinegar, 100 ml water, salt, sugar and lemon zest in a saucepan and bring to the boil. Simmer for 3 minutes, then let cool.

Put the salmon fillet in a shallow, non-reactive container with the shallots and dill. Pour over the pickling liquid and cover tightly. Leave in the refrigerator for 2–3 days, turning the salmon once a day.

To assemble the salad, remove the salmon from the pickling liquid and slice it into thin strips. Arrange the salmon on serving plates with a few of the pickled shallots.

Slice the fennel and cucumber very thinly, using a mandoline if you have one, and put in a bowl. Chop the green fennel fronds, if available, very finely and add 3 tablespoonfuls to the bowl.

In a small bowl, whisk together the lemon juice, mustard and oil and season to taste with salt and pepper. Just before serving, toss the dressing through the fennel and cucumber salad and arrange a little on top of the salmon. Drizzle with extra oil to serve, if liked.

Salad Niçoise is traditionally made with tinned tuna, but fresh tuna steaks make it extra special and more filling. Of course you can always use good-quality tinned or bottled tuna if you prefer.

salad niçoise with fresh tuna

8 small waxy potatoes

4 eggs

200 g green beans, trimmed

4 x 160-g tuna steaks

2 teaspoons olive oil

150 g crisp lettuce

4 tomatoes, cut into wedges

16 black olives

2 tablespoons white wine vinegar

1 teaspoon Dijon mustard

4 tablespoons extra virgin olive oil

sea salt and freshly ground black pepper

a ridged griddle pan

SERVES 4

Put the potatoes in a large saucepan of water and bring to the boil then reduce the heat and cook until tender. Drain and halve or quarter if necessary.

Put the eggs in a saucepan and cover with tepid water. Bring to the boil and boil for 4 minutes for medium and 6 minutes for hard-boiled, as preferred. Cool under cold running water, peel and quarter.

Bring a saucepan of water to the boil, add the beans and cook until tender. Drain and refresh with iced water.

Heat a ridged griddle pan to hot. Rub the tuna with olive oil and season with salt and pepper. Cook in the pan for 2 minutes on each side, remove from the heat and leave to rest for 5 minutes. Cut into pieces.

Arrange the lettuce, tomatoes, olives, potatoes, egg quarters, beans and tuna on serving plates.

In a bowl, whisk together the vinegar and mustard and season to taste with salt and pepper. Whisk in the extra virgin olive oil until well blended. Pour over each salad just before serving.

This salad uses lean beef fillet, but is also good with other lean meat such as venison. The fillet is very rare; if you want to cook it through, cook in an oven preheated to 180°C (350°F) Gas 4 for 15 minutes before placing in the second marinade.

twice-marinated beef, asparagus, pepper and bean salad

1 tablespoon Sichuan peppercorns*

2 garlic cloves, chopped

1 teaspoon sea salt

2 teaspoons groundnut oil

400-g piece of beef fillet

2 tablespoons rice vinegar (black)*

2 tablespoons Japanese* or golden soy sauce

2 teaspoons sesame oil

2 teaspoons sugar

½ teaspoon red dried chilli flakes

4 peppers, 2 red and 2 yellow

500 g asparagus, trimmed and cut into 3-cm pieces

250 g frozen edamame beans*

60 g beansprouts

sweet soy dressing

1 tablespoon Japanese* or golden soy sauce

1 tablespoon freshly squeezed lemon juice

1 tablespoon rice vinegar*

1 tablespoon sugar

½ teaspoon crushed fresh red chilli

SERVES 4

*see glossary pages 140–141

Put the Sichuan peppercorns, garlic and salt in a mortar and pestle or mini food processor and grind or process to a paste, adding the groundnut oil gradually until it is incorporated. Rub this mixture all over the beef and leave for 5 minutes to marinate.

In a medium-sized non-reactive bowl, mix together the vinegar, soy sauce, sesame oil, sugar and chilli flakes.

Heat a griddle pan to very hot, add the beef and sear on each side for 1 minute until browned all over. Remove from the heat and immediately put in the marinade, turning to coat well. Let cool, cover and refrigerate for at least 1 hour, but preferably overnight, turning occasionally.

Heat the grill to very hot. Cut each pepper lengthways into 3 and remove the stems and seeds. Cook skin-side up under the preheated grill for about 10 minutes until blackened and soft. Put in a bowl, cover with a lid or clingfilm and let steam for 10 minutes. Peel off all the blackened skin and cut the flesh into 1-cm strips. Put on a serving dish.

Cook the asparagus in boiling water for 3 minutes until tender, then quickly refresh with iced water and drain well. Add to the peppers.

Cook the edamame beans in boiling water for 3 minutes, then quickly refresh with iced water. Remove the beans from the pods and add to the peppers and asparagus.

Put the beansprouts in a sieve and pour over boiling water to blanch, then quickly refresh with iced water and drain well. Add to the peppers, asparagus and edamame beans.

To make the sweet soy dressing, combine the soy sauce, lemon juice, vinegar, sugar and chilli in a small bowl. Stir until the sugar has dissolved.

Just before serving, slice the beef as thinly as possible and add to the salad, pour over the dressing and toss. Serve immediately.

roast duck, sausage, sweet potato and cherry salad

4 duck legs

3 tablespoons olive oil

½ teaspoon ground cinnamon

3 sweet potatoes (about 200 g each), peeled

1 teaspoon sea salt flakes

8 thin sausages, duck or pork

1 tablespoon sherry vinegar or cider vinegar

finely grated zest of 1 orange and 2 tablespoons freshly squeezed juice

1 tablespoon runny honey

1 teaspoon Dijon mustard

4 tablespoons extra virgin olive oil

1 frisée lettuce, leaves separated

24 cherries, halved and stoned

SERVES 4

A delicious festive salad. The frisée adds a slight bitterness that works well, but you can substitute any other type of lettuce.

Preheat the oven to 180°C (350°F) Gas 4.

Slash the duck legs a few times through the flesh. Put 2 tablespoons of the olive oil in a small bowl and whisk in the cinnamon. Use your fingers to rub the oil into the duck. Put the duck in a roasting tin and roast in the preheated oven for 1 hour, turning occasionally.

Cut the sweet potatoes into 2-cm cubes and toss in a bowl with the remaining olive oil and ½ teaspoon of the salt flakes.

Remove the duck from the roasting tin and set aside to cool. Pour most of the rendered fat off the roasting tin and discard (or reserve for roasting potatoes another time). Add the sausages and sweet potatoes to the roasting tin and coat with the little fat left from the duck. Roast for 30 minutes, stirring twice. Remove from the oven and let cool. Cut the sausages into quarters. Slice the meat from the duck legs.

In a bowl, whisk together the vinegar, orange zest and juice, honey, mustard and remaining ½ teaspoon salt flakes. Slowly whisk in the extra virgin olive oil until incorporated.

Arrange the frisée on a serving plate. Top with the duck, sausages, sweet potatoes and cherries. Pour over the dressing and serve immediately.

pork and lentil salad

200 g Puy or French
green lentils

1 teaspoon Dijon mustard

2 tablespoons balsamic vinegar

½ teaspoon sea salt

½ teaspoon freshly ground
black pepper

4 tablespoons extra virgin
olive oil

250 g button mushrooms

1 tablespoon olive oil

finely grated zest of 1 lemon

2 garlic cloves, crushed

2 tablespoons rosemary
needles, chopped

350-g piece of pork eye fillet

100 ml red wine

100 g baby spinach leaves,
washed

16 cherry tomatoes, halved

SERVES 4

This is a hearty and delicious salad. The Puy lentils give a lovely nutty texture and a rustic feel to the dish.

Put the lentils in a saucepan with plenty of cold water. Bring to the boil, then reduce to a simmer and cook for 20 minutes. Drain and set aside.

In a large bowl, whisk together the mustard, vinegar and ¼ teaspoon each of salt and pepper, then whisk in the extra virgin olive oil. Add the mushrooms and warm lentils and toss well to coat. Set aside to marinate.

In a small bowl, mix together the olive oil, lemon zest, garlic, rosemary and remaining ¼ teaspoon each of salt and pepper. Rub this mixture all over the pork fillets.

Heat a frying pan to medium, add the pork and cook for 5 minutes on each side. Remove the pork from the pan to a chopping board and leave to rest for 5 minutes, then slice thinly.

Pour the wine into the hot frying pan and let it bubble, stirring in any marinade left in the pan. Pour this over the lentils and mushrooms.

Add the sliced pork to the lentils and mushrooms along with the spinach leaves and cherry tomatoes and toss to combine. Serve immediately.

sweet curried salad of cheese and greens

½–1 teaspoon curry powder, to taste

2 tablespoons mango chutney

4 tablespoons mayonnaise

1 tablespoon cider vinegar

¼ teaspoon sea salt

2 small leeks

3 celery sticks, sliced

½ iceberg lettuce, sliced

a bunch of chives, chopped

70 g cashew nuts, roasted and chopped

150 g mild cheese, such as Edam, firm paneer, young Leyden or Colby

½ teaspoon nigella seeds*

warm bread, to serve

SERVES 4

see glossary pages 140–141

This unusual combination is a total mishmash of cuisines, but somehow works brilliantly and tastes fantastic served with warmed Indian-style bread such as naan. You could substitute the cheese for cooked chicken if you prefer.

In a bowl, whisk together ½ teaspoon of the curry powder, the chutney, mayonnaise, vinegar and salt. Taste and add more curry powder if liked. Set aside.

Wash the leeks thoroughly and slice as thinly as you can. Either use the leeks raw (as I like to) or blanch them in boiling water if you prefer a milder flavour. Place in a serving bowl with the celery, lettuce, chives and cashew nuts.

Cut the cheese into 1-cm cubes and add to the salad. Pour in the dressing and mix well.

Heat a frying pan over medium heat, add the nigella seeds and toast, tossing in the pan, for about 1 minute until just fragrant.

Sprinkle the nigella seeds over the salad. Serve immediately with plenty of warm bread.

To make a meat-free version of this salad, simply replace the livers with quartered mushrooms. For an extra-rich salad, add a handful of chopped, crisply fried bacon.

warm chicken livers with
watercress and ciabatta

3 tablespoons olive oil

1 onion, thinly sliced

6 slices of ciabatta bread

500 g watercress, thick stems removed

500 g chicken livers, halved

125 ml Marsala or cream sherry

1 tablespoon wholegrain mustard

1 tablespoon chopped sage

sea salt and freshly ground black pepper

extra virgin olive oil, for drizzling

SERVES 4

Heat 1 tablespoon of the olive oil over medium-low heat in a large frying pan. Add the onion and sauté for 20 minutes until soft and turning golden. Set aside.

Preheat the grill to hot. Brush the ciabatta with 1 tablespoon of the olive oil and grill until brown on both sides. Tear into bite-sized pieces. Arrange on serving plates with the watercress.

Carefully sort through the livers, cutting off any green specks of bile and pulling away sinew and connective tissue, then gently rinse.

Heat the frying pan to hot and add the remaining tablespoon of olive oil and the livers. Cook for 3 minutes, stirring, until just done. Transfer the livers to a warmed plate. Add the Marsala to the pan and bring to the boil. Let boil for 1 minute, scraping the pan and stirring until the mixture has reduced by half.

Return the livers to the pan with the mustard, sage and a little salt and pepper, and toss in the pan for 30 seconds.

Pile the hot livers onto the watercress and ciabatta, top with the onion and drizzle with a little extra virgin olive oil. Serve immediately.

puri salad

80 g raw, unsalted peanuts

50 g long grain rice

4 waxy potatoes

60 ml natural yoghurt

2 tablespoons tamarind chutney

2 tablespoons freshly squeezed lemon or lime juice

½ iceberg lettuce

1 small (Lebanese) or ½ large cucumber, deseeded and chopped

1 red onion, finely chopped

2 large red chillies, deseeded and chopped

70 g dried dates, chopped

40 g sev* or bhuja mix*

leaves from a large bunch of coriander

2 teaspoons chaat masala* (optional)

sea salt

SERVES 4

see glossary pages 140–141

Bhel puri is my favourite Indian street food – a near perfect combination of crunchy, cool, spicy, sweet and savoury flavours. This recipe captures the essence of puri in a salad.

Preheat the oven to 150°C (300°F) Gas 2.

Spread the peanuts out in an even layer over a baking tray. Roast in the preheated oven for 20–25 minutes, stirring occasionally, until the nuts are just smelling toasted.

Put the roasted nuts in a clean tea towel and rub vigorously until the skins come loose. Shake or blow the loosened skins away, and continue rubbing the nuts until they are free from skins. Chop the peanuts roughly and set aside.

Heat a wok or frying pan to very hot. Add the rice and cook, shaking the pan constantly, for about 1 minute, until the rice is golden and pops. Transfer to a mortar and pestle and pound to a coarse powder. Transfer to a bowl and let cool.

Put the potatoes in a large saucepan of water and bring to the boil. Reduce the heat and cook until tender. Drain well and let cool before cutting into small cubes.

In a large bowl, whisk together the yoghurt, chutney and lemon juice and season to taste with salt. Add the lettuce, cucumber, onion, chillies, dates and potatoes and toss.

Arrange the salad on a serving plate and sprinkle with the rice, sev, roasted peanuts, coriander and chaat masala, if using.

2 garlic cloves, crushed

finely grated zest of 1 lemon

1 teaspoon allspice
berries, crushed

2 tablespoons thyme leaves

½ teaspoon sea salt flakes

½ teaspoon freshly ground
black pepper

3 tablespoons olive oil

4 skin-on chicken breasts or leg
and thigh pieces

6 courgettes

100 g bulghur wheat

leaves from a small bunch of
flat leaf parsley

4 tablespoons pomegranate
seeds (optional)

pomegranate vinaigrette

1 tablespoon white
wine vinegar

2 tablespoons pomegranate
molasses*

3 tablespoons extra virgin
olive oil

SERVES 4

*see glossary pages 140–141

chicken, courgette and bulghur salad with pomegranate vinaigrette

Serve this with plenty of warmed Middle Eastern-style flatbreads. As an extra touch, you could crumble feta cheese over the salad.

Preheat the oven to 180°C (350°F) Gas 4.

In a small bowl, mix together the garlic, lemon zest, allspice, thyme, ¼ teaspoon each of the salt and pepper and 2 tablespoons olive oil.

Put the chicken pieces in a dish and loosen the skin by sliding your hand between the skin and flesh. Rub the oil mixture under the skin. Roast in the preheated oven for 30 minutes for breasts and 50 minutes for leg and thigh pieces. Let cool, then slice or tear the meat into pieces.

Cut the courgettes in half, then slice each half into quarters lengthways. Toss in a bowl with the remaining tablespoon of olive oil and ¼ teaspoon each of salt and pepper. Place in a roasting dish and roast for 20 minutes.

Put the bulghur wheat in a bowl and cover with cold water. Leave to soak for 30 minutes until tender but not too soft. Drain well and press down hard on the wheat with the back of a large spoon to squeeze out any excess water.

To make the vinaigrette. whisk together the vinegar and pomegranate molasses in a small bowl, then whisk in the extra virgin olive oil.

Arrange the bulghur wheat, chicken, courgettes and parsley on a serving dish and pour over the dressing. Toss lightly, then scatter over the pomegranate seeds, if using.

salsas and dips

tomato, green olive and preserved lemon salsa

6 large tomatoes

100 g green olives, stoned

rind of 1 preserved lemon*, rinsed

2 tablespoons harissa paste*

2 tablespoons olive oil

sea salt

flatbreads or pita crisps, to serve

MAKES ABOUT 750 ML

see glossary pages 140–141

This is a spicy salsa inspired by Moroccan ingredients and made with harissa, a pungent, hot North African chilli and spice paste. Serve it with seafood, chicken, lamb, potatoes or flatbreads.

Cut a small cross in the base of each tomato and put in a heatproof bowl. Pour over boiling water to cover and leave for 1–2 minutes. Remove from the water and let cool. When cool enough to handle, carefully peel off the skins and discard.

Cut the tomatoes into quarters, scoop out the seeds and discard. Finely chop the flesh and put in a bowl. Chop the olives and preserved lemon rind very finely. Add to the tomatoes with the harissa paste and oil and mix well. Season with salt and set aside for a few hours before using. The salsa will keep in the refrigerator for 3 days.

smoky pepper and aubergine salsa

2 red peppers

1 aubergine

3 tablespoons olive oil

1 red onion, finely chopped

3 garlic cloves, chopped

1–2 teaspoons minced red chilli

1 teaspoon sugar

½ teaspoon sea salt

1 tablespoon freshly squeezed lemon juice

a small bunch of flat leaf parsley, chopped

2 tablespoons chopped dill

2 teaspoons ground sumac*

MAKES ABOUT 625 ML

see glossary pages 140–141

This smoky-flavoured salsa is great with any barbecued food or as a condiment on burgers and sausages.

Roast the aubergine and red peppers directly over the flame of a gas burner or barbecue, or put under a preheated grill, turning regularly, until completely blackened and soft. Put them in a large bowl, cover with a lid or clingfilm and let them steam for 10 minutes. Remove and peel off all the blackened skin and discard. Remove the stems and seeds from the peppers and chop the flesh very finely. Cut the stem off the aubergine and chop the flesh very finely.

Heat 1 tablespoon of the oil in a frying pan, add the onion and garlic and sauté for 5 minutes until soft. Transfer to a large bowl with the peppers, aubergine, remaining 2 tablespoons oil, chilli, sugar, salt, lemon juice, parsley and dill and mix well.

Place in a serving bowl and sprinkle with the sumac. The salsa will keep in the refrigerator for 3 days.

rocket and fennel salsa verde

2 teaspoons fennel seeds

1 garlic clove

1 tablespoon small drained capers

3 anchovy fillets

25 g rocket, chopped

2 tablespoons chopped flat leaf parsley

1 tablespoon freshly squeezed lemon juice

4 tablespoons olive oil

sea salt and freshly ground black pepper

MAKES ABOUT 125 ML

A sharp, pungent and versatile spooning sauce, salsa verde is the perfect foil to rich foods such as ham, pork and salmon. It is also great served with fish, lamb, chicken, potatoes or pasta.

Heat a frying pan over medium heat and add the fennel seeds. Toast them, stirring, for about 1 minute until fragrant. Let cool. Transfer to a mortar and pestle and grind to a rough powder.

Combine the ground fennel seeds, garlic, capers and anchovies in a small bowl and pound until blended. Alternatively, blend them in a mini food processor. Add the rocket, parsley, lemon juice and oil and mix to combine until you have a coarse sauce. Season to taste with salt and pepper. The salsa will keep in the refrigerator for up to 1 week, but it will quickly start to discolour, so is best used when freshly made.

caramelized pineapple and chilli salsa

½ fresh pineapple

1 teaspoon caster sugar

2 limes

1 small red onion, finely chopped

3 large, mild red chillies, deseeded and finely chopped

3 large, mild green chillies, deseeded and finely chopped

a small bunch of mint, finely chopped

MAKES ABOUT 600 ML

This tangy, sweet and spicy salsa is full of chillies, so it is important to use large, mild varieties. Enjoy it with barbecued food, chicken, pork sausages, ham or firm, robust fish such as tuna or swordfish.

Cut the skin off the pineapple and discard. Cut the flesh into 1.5-cm slices. Sprinkle with sugar.

Heat a frying pan until hot, add the pineapple and cook for 2–3 minutes on each side until caramelized. Remove from the pan and let cool. Chop the pineapple and put in a bowl with any juices.

Cut the top and bottom from the limes and slice off the rind and any white pith. Carefully slice between each segment and remove the flesh. Chop the flesh and add to the pineapple along with the onion, chillies and mint, then mix to combine. The salsa will keep in the refrigerator for 3 days.

sweet chilli and tomato salsa

2 tablespoons sesame seeds

1 teaspoon Sichuan peppercorns*

a small bunch of coriander, stems and leaves

3 garlic cloves, peeled

2 large, mild red chillies, stems removed

3-cm piece fresh ginger, peeled

100 g caster sugar

2 tablespoons freshly squeezed lime juice

1 tablespoon soy sauce

4 tomatoes, chopped

MAKES ABOUT 400 ML

see glossary pages 140–141

This is an Asian-inspired salsa with a sweet and spicy flavour. It can be served as a dip with rice or prawn crackers or vegetable crisps, or as an accompaniment to shellfish, fish, chicken, pork or duck.

Heat a frying pan to medium, add the sesame seeds and toast, tossing the pan, until golden. Set aside.

In the same frying pan, toast the Sichuan peppercorns for 3 minutes, stirring, until just fragrant. Let cool, transfer to a mortar and pestle and roughly grind. Put the Sichuan pepper in a mini food processor with the coriander stems, garlic, chillies and ginger and process to a paste.

Put the sugar in a saucepan with a little water and bring to the boil, stirring until dissolved. Boil undisturbed for 1 minute, stir in the chilli and ginger paste and remove from the heat. Let cool.

In a bowl, mix together the sugar syrup and chilli paste mixture, lime juice, soy sauce, chopped tomatoes, coriander leaves and sesame seeds. The salsa will keep in the refrigerator for 3 days.

roast garlic, paprika and sherry alioli

1 whole garlic bulb

2 egg yolks

1 tablespoon sherry vinegar

¼ teaspoon sea salt

¼ teaspoon smoked paprika

190 ml light-flavoured oil, such as grapeseed or vegetable

1 tablespoon sherry

MAKES ABOUT 200 ML

Spanish-style alioli is great as a dipping sauce for seafood and vegetables or a good accompaniment to barbecued vegetables and meats. I have given the hand-whisking method, but the alioli can be made in the small bowl of a food processor.

Preheat the oven to 180°C (350°F) Gas 4.

Cut 1 cm off the top of the garlic bulb and discard. Loosely wrap the garlic in foil and roast in the preheated oven for 45 minutes until very soft. Let cool, then press the softened cloves from the skins. Crush the cloves on a chopping board with the side of a large knife to form a paste.

In a bowl, whisk together the garlic with the egg yolks, vinegar, salt and paprika. Add the oil, drop by drop, whisking continuously until emulsified and thick. Finally whisk in the sherry. The alioli will keep in the refrigerator for 2–3 days.

warm pinto bean and cheese dip

200 g dried pinto beans

1 onion, quartered

a small bunch of thyme

1 bay leaf

3 red peppers

400 ml passata (Italian sieved tomatoes)

1 tablespoon olive oil

2 garlic cloves, chopped

70 g pickled jalapeño peppers

½ teaspoon sea salt

150 g mature Cheddar cheese, grated

2 teaspoons plain flour

taco or pita crisps OR warm tortillas and vegetable crudités, to serve

SERVES 6–8

A great dip for a crowd, you can make this up to the point when you add in the cheese, then simply reheat and add the cheese just before serving. Note that you'll need to soak the beans overnight.

Soak the beans in cold water overnight. Drain, put in a large saucepan with the onion, thyme and bay leaf and cover with plenty of water. Bring to the boil and continue to boil for 15 minutes. Reduce the heat and simmer for 1 hour, partially covered, until the beans are tender. Drain the cooked beans, reserving about 100 ml of the cooking liquid. Remove the bay leaf and any thyme stalks.

Roast the peppers directly over the flame of a gas burner or barbecue, or under a preheated grill, turning regularly, until completely blackened. Put in a large bowl and cover with cling film. Let steam for about 10 minutes, then peel off the skins and discard. Split the peppers and remove the stems and seeds. Put in a food processor and blend to a purée with the beans and passata.

Heat the oil in a heavy-based saucepan over medium heat, add the garlic and sauté for 1 minute. Stir in the jalapeño peppers and then the bean purée and salt and simmer for 10 minutes, adding a little of the reserved bean cooking liquid if it gets too thick.

Lower the heat to very low. Toss the cheese with the flour and add to the bean mixture, stirring constantly until well blended. The dip is best served warm, but it will keep in the refrigerator for up to 3 days and can be eaten cold.

Hummus is simple and fun to make at home. It's also versatile, as you can flavour it to suit you. For an extra-special, creamy hummus, peel the skin from the cooked chickpeas, an arduous task, but you'll be amazed at the results.

hummus bi tahini

150 g dried chickpeas or
1½ x 420-g tins chickpeas,
drained

60 ml freshly squeezed
lemon juice

1–2 garlic cloves

5 tablespoons tahini*

½ teaspoon sea salt

extra virgin olive oil, for drizzling
(optional)

vegetable crudités and
flatbreads, to serve

MAKES ABOUT 600 ML

*see glossary pages 140–141

If using dried chickpeas, soak them overnight or for at least 12 hours. Drain and put in a large saucepan. Cover with about 3 times the volume of water. Bring to the boil, reduce to a simmer and cook for 1½ hours or until tender, topping up the water if necessary. Drain the chickpeas and reserve about 20 ml of the cooking liquid. Let cool. (At this point you can rub the chickpeas to loosen the skins and discard.)

Put the cooked chickpeas in a food processor with the lemon juice, garlic, tahini and salt. Process to a smooth purée, adding some of the cooking liquid (or a little water if you are using tinned chickpeas) to achieve the desired consistency – usually about 3 tablespoons.

Serve drizzled with olive oil, if liked. The hummus will keep in the refrigerator for 5 days.

Variations:

Roast garlic hummus Preheat the oven to 180°C (350°F) Gas 4. Cut about 1 cm off the top of a whole bulb of garlic and discard. Loosely wrap the garlic in foil and roast in the preheated oven for about 45 minutes until very soft. Let cool. Squeeze the soft garlic cloves out of their skins and add to the chickpeas when you purée them.

Grilled vegetable hummus On a barbecue or in a griddle pan, cook slices of red pepper, aubergine, pumpkin or courgette that have been tossed with a little olive oil. Add to the chickpeas when you purée them.

Minted pea or bean hummus add 130 g cooked peas or cooked and shelled broad beans and 2 tablespoons chopped mint to the chickpeas when you purée them.

tzatziki

½ cucumber, deseeded and grated

2 teaspoons sea salt

1 garlic clove, crushed (optional)

150 ml Greek yoghurt

freshly squeezed juice of ½ lemon

MAKES ABOUT 250 ML

Greek tzatziki is a versatile, low-fat dip and it also makes a great salad dressing or accompaniment to barbecued chicken and fish or roast Mediterranean-style vegetables.

Mix the grated cucumber and salt together and let stand for 10 minutes. Put the cucumber in the centre of a clean tea towel, gather up the edges and twist to squeeze as much moisture out as possible. Put the cucumber in a bowl with the remaining ingredients and stir to combine. The tzatziki will keep in the refrigerator for 3 days.

Variations:

Beetroot tzatziki Add 1 medium raw or 2 bottled beetroot, grated, and 2 tablespoons chopped chives to the mixture. This makes a great accompaniment to boiled new potatoes.

Spiced tzatziki Put 2 teaspoons cumin seeds and 2 teaspoons coriander seeds in a hot frying pan and heat, stirring, for about 30 seconds until fragrant. Transfer to a mortar and pestle and grind to a powder. Add to the tzatziki along with 1 teaspoon paprika.

Olive tzatziki Stir 75–100 g finely chopped stoned black or green olives into the yoghurt and cucumber mixture.

guacamole

3 medium, ripe avocados, halved, stoned and peeled

2 tablespoons freshly squeezed lime juice

1 small red onion, very finely chopped

1–2 green chillies, very finely chopped

1 tomato, deseeded and finely chopped

sea salt

tortilla chips or bread sticks, to serve

MAKES 500 ML

This popular Mexican dip can be made in many ways. This recipe contains all the popular ingredients, but feel free to leave out any you don't like. Adjust the chillies according to your taste.

Put the avocado flesh in a bowl with the lime juice and crush to a rough purée with a fork (if you like a smooth purée, you can blend the avocado and lime juice together in a food processor, then transfer to a bowl).

Add the onion, chillies and tomato and mix until combined. Season to taste with salt. The guacamole will discolour quickly, so is best eaten on the day of making.

Variations:

Herbed guacamole Add 2 teaspoons each of finely chopped coriander, mint and parsley to the guacamole for a pungent, refreshing dip.

Feta and avocado dip Add 75 g finely crumbled feta cheese to the guacamole. This is great served with pita crisps.

mushroom bagna cauda

400 ml single cream

2 teaspoons olive oil

1 tablespoon butter

250 g fresh mushrooms, finely chopped

¼ teaspoon sea salt

50–75 g (about 12) anchovy fillets, finely chopped

4–5 garlic cloves, crushed

vegetable crudités and/or bread, to serve

MAKES ABOUT 300 ML

This mushroom version of Piedmont's classic hot anchovy and garlic dip is delicious with vegetable crudités. It is traditionally served in a small dish set over flame to keep it warm but you can also serve it in a warmed bowl.

Bring the cream to the boil in a small saucepan and, stirring, reduce by half.

Heat the olive oil and butter in a medium saucepan set over medium heat. Add the mushrooms and salt and cook for about 6 minutes, stirring occasionally, until the mushrooms are tender. (You may need to add a little water to help them cook.)

Add the anchovies and garlic and cook briefly, mashing together. Stir in the reduced cream and heat to hot but not boiling. Serve with vegetables and or bread for dipping. Best eaten on the day of making.

artichoke tarator

2 slices of day-old bread,
crusts removed

6 tinned artichoke hearts,
drained

freshly squeezed juice of
1 lemon

3–4 garlic cloves, crushed

½ teaspoon sea salt

70 g blanched almonds,
finely chopped

4 tablespoons olive oil, plus
extra for drizzling

toasted flaked almonds,
to serve

MAKES ABOUT 500 ML

Tarator is a fabulous garlic and nut dip, and this version has artichokes to make it extra special. Perfect as a dip with vegetable crudités – it goes especially well with endive. In Turkey it is served as a spooning sauce with grilled white fish, such as sea bass.

Put the bread in a sieve and pour over boiling water; when cool enough to handle, squeeze out any excess water.

Chop the artichoke hearts and put in a food processor or large pestle and mortar with the bread, lemon juice, garlic, salt and almonds. Blend together, adding the oil slowly to combine.

To serve, drizzle with extra oil and scatter with the flaked almonds. The tarator will keep in the refrigerator for up to 3 days.

relishes, pickles
and sauces

tomato, lemon and courgette relish

2 small lemons

500 g courgettes, finely chopped

2 red or white onions, finely chopped

4 tablespoons sea salt

1 kg tomatoes, chopped

150 g sugar

375 ml white wine vinegar or cider vinegar

1 tablespoon white mustard seeds

1 teaspoon dill seeds or celery seeds

¼ teaspoon turmeric

MAKES ABOUT 1250 ML

Pickled or preserved lemons develop such a unique and wonderful flavour that is captured in this tomato and courgette relish. It makes a great accompaniment to sausages, lamb, chicken and hard cheeses, but it really goes with practically anything!

Carefully cut the rind from the lemons, with a very thin layer of white pith. Finely chop and put in a glass or ceramic bowl with the juice from 1 of the lemons. Put the courgettes and onions in separate bowls. Sprinkle each with the salt, cover and leave at room temperature overnight. When ready to make the relish, rinse well with cold water and drain thoroughly.

Put the tomatoes, sugar and vinegar in a large saucepan and bring to the boil, stirring constantly to dissolve the sugar. Reduce to a simmer and cook for 1 hour, stirring occasionally, until thick. Bring back to the boil and add the drained lemon rind, courgettes and onions with the mustard seeds, dill seeds and turmeric. Cook for 5 minutes. Spoon into sterilized jars and seal. The relish will keep for up to 1 year if sealed correctly

NOTE Always sterilize preserving jars before use. Wash them in hot, soapy water and rinse in boiling water. Place in a large saucepan and then cover with hot water. With the lid on, bring the water to the boil and continue boiling for 15 minutes. Turn off the heat, then leave the jars in the hot water until just before they are to be filled. Invert the jars onto clean kitchen paper to dry. Sterilize the lids for 5 minutes, by boiling, or according to the manufacturers' instructions. Jars should be filled and sealed while they are still hot.

crunchy sweetcorn and pepper relish

3 peppers, 1 red, 1 yellow and 1 orange

sweetcorn kernels from 2 corn-on-the-cobs

1 red or white onion, chopped

4 tablespoons sea salt

1 teaspoon white mustard seeds

½ teaspoon cumin seeds

½ teaspoon coriander seeds

½ teaspoon whole black peppercorns

6 small dried chillies

375 ml white (distilled) vinegar

115 g sugar

¼ teaspoon turmeric

MAKES ABOUT 900 ML

Fresh sweetcorn and colourful peppers make such a vibrant relish and the crunchy texture also adds appeal. You can serve the relish the day you make it, but it's even better preserved.

Remove the stems from the peppers and discard. Cut the peppers into 2-cm dice and put in a colander with the sweetcorn and onion. Toss with the salt and leave for 2–4 hours. Rinse well with cold water and shake dry.

Heat a saucepan over medium heat and add the mustard, cumin and coriander seeds, peppercorns and chillies. Cook, stirring, for 1 minute until fragrant. Add the vinegar, sugar and turmeric and bring to the boil, stirring to dissolve the sugar.

Add the rinsed sweetcorn, peppers and onion to the vinegar mixture. Cover and bring to the boil.

If using immediately, let cool, stirring occasionally. To preserve, fill sterilized jars with the relish while it is still hot and seal (see note on page 127). The relish will keep for up to 2 months if sealed correctly

beetroot and horseradish relish

2 tablespoons sugar

2 tablespoons balsamic vinegar

300 g raw beetroot, peeled

1 tablespoon bottled horseradish

MAKES 300 ML

If you're serving burgers, sausages or steaks (even salmon steaks), here is a very quick accompaniment that will transform the meal. Fresh, raw beetroot is best, but you can substitute pre-cooked.

To make the relish, put the sugar and vinegar in a small saucepan and bring to the boil, stirring. Boil for 1 minute, then remove from the heat. Grate the beetroot into a bowl and combine with the horseradish and vinegar syrup. The relish will keep in the refrigerator for up to 1 week.

red cabbage and currant pickle

3 tablespoons olive oil

½ small red cabbage, thinly sliced

60 ml red wine

3 tablespoons brown sugar

60 ml balsamic vinegar

35 g currants

35 g pine nuts

MAKES ABOUT 625 ML

This instant sweet-and-sour pickle is great served with rich meats such as sausages or with vegetables.

Heat the oil in a large frying pan over low to medium heat. Add the cabbage, cover and cook for 5 minutes. Turn up the heat to high, add the wine and let it bubble, then add the sugar, vinegar and currants. Cook, stirring, for 5 minutes.

Heat a frying pan to medium, add the pine nuts and toast, stirring, until golden. Stir the toasted pine nuts into the pickle. Let cool and refrigerate until needed. The pickle will keep in the refrigerator for up to 2 weeks.

crisp apple and ginger pickle

½ teaspoon fenugreek seeds

½ teaspoon black mustard seeds

½ teaspoon turmeric

½ teaspoon sea salt

1 tablespoon crushed chilli paste

1 tablespoon mustard oil or plain-flavoured oil, such as grapeseed

2 green apples, cored and cut into 2-cm pieces

5-cm piece of fresh ginger, peeled and grated

70 g raisins (optional)

MAKES ABOUT 500 ML

Serving a very hot, fresh pickle is a great way to let people add more heat if they like it. Raisins add a sweetness that complements the spice, but they can be omitted. This pickle is especially good with pork, sausages, chicken and root vegetables.

Heat a frying pan over medium heat and add the fenugreek and mustard seeds. Cook, stirring constantly, for about 1 minute, until fragrant. Transfer to a mortar and pestle with the turmeric and salt and grind together. Add the chilli paste and oil and pound to make a paste.

Put the apple pieces, ginger and raisins, if using, in a bowl and stir in the paste until well combined. Cover and refrigerate until needed. The pickle will keep in the refrigerator for up to 2 days.

coriander chutney

1 garlic clove, crushed

4 large, mild green chillies, deseeded and chopped

3-cm piece of fresh ginger, peeled and chopped

a very large bunch of coriander, leaves and stems chopped

1 teaspoon sugar

1 tablespoon freshly squeezed lemon or lime juice

1 tablespoon rapeseed (canola) oil

MAKES ABOUT 125 ML

A traditional Indian fresh chutney that can be served with anything or it works well combined with yoghurt and offered as a dip.

Put the garlic, chillies, ginger, coriander and sugar in a small food processor or a large mortar and pestle and grind to a paste.

While mixing, slowly add the lemon juice and oil. If necessary, mix in sufficient water to make a thick but spreadable paste.

The chutney is best eaten immediately, as it will quickly discolour.

onion marmalade

3 white or red onions

1 tablespoon olive oil

1 tablespoon brown sugar

1 tablespoon red wine vinegar, cider vinegar or balsamic vinegar

2 teaspoons wholegrain mustard

sea salt and freshly ground black pepper

MAKES ABOUT 250 ML

This soft, sticky onion marmalade is great with meat pâtés and terrines, a cheese plate or ploughman's lunch, or even with sausages and mash.

Peel the onions and trim the root end, but keep it attached. Cut each onion into 12 wedges.

Heat the oil in a frying pan over low heat, add the onions and gently cook for 1 hour until they are very soft but only just turning brown. Raise the heat to medium and stir in the sugar and vinegar. Cook, stirring, for a few minutes, then stir in the mustard. Season with salt and pepper. Let cool. The marmalade is best eaten immediately, but it will keep in the refrigerator for up to 1 week.

Home-made tomato ketchup captures the true flavour of ripe tomatoes in season. Slow-roasting the tomatoes results in a more intense flavour, but one that is not as full-on as barbecue sauce.

roast tomato ketchup

2 kg tomatoes

3 teaspoons sea salt

leaves from a small bunch of thyme

2 tablespoons olive oil

1 white onion, chopped

1 teaspoon allspice berries

½ teaspoon whole cloves

½ teaspoon black peppercorns

400 g sugar

1 teaspoon dry mustard powder

500 ml cider vinegar

MAKES ABOUT 1.5 LITRES

Preheat the oven to 150°C (300°F) Gas 2.

Cut the tomatoes in half and arrange cut-side up in a roasting tin. Sprinkle with 2 teaspoons of the salt and all the thyme leaves and drizzle with 1 tablespoon of the oil. Roast in the preheated oven for 1½ hours.

Heat the remaining 1 tablespoon of oil in a large saucepan over medium heat, add the onion and sauté for 10 minutes until golden.

Put the allspice, cloves and peppercorns in a mortar and pestle and grind to a powder. Add to the onion and cook for 1 minute. Add the roasted tomatoes, sugar, mustard powder, vinegar and remaining 1 teaspoon salt and bring to the boil. Adjust the heat to a steady low boil and cook for 30 minutes, uncovered, stirring occasionally.

Blend to a thick sauce using a stick blender or transfer to a blender. Pour into sterilized bottles and seal (see note on page 127).

The ketchup will keep for up to 1 year if properly sealed and stored in a cool, dark place.

nuoc cham

3 chillies, sliced (leave the seeds in for a hot sauce)

1 garlic clove, finely chopped

3 teaspoons palm* or brown sugar

freshly squeezed juice of 2 limes

2 tablespoons rice vinegar*

3 tablespoons Thai fish sauce*

MAKES ABOUT 125 ML

*see glossary pages 140–141

Nuoc cham is on every table at every meal in Vietnam – it goes with everything and is a great way to enliven simple foods. You can play around with quantities of ingredients to suit your taste, as there are many interpretations of the same basic recipe.

In a bowl, whisk together the chillies, garlic, sugar, lime juice, vinegar and fish sauce until the sugar has dissolved.

Set aside for at least 15 minutes before serving to allow the flavours to develop. The sauce is best eaten on the day it is made.

macadamia and chilli sauce

1 tablespoon macadamia or groundnut oil

1 teaspoon blachan*

2 garlic cloves, crushed

4 shallots, finely chopped

125 ml coconut cream

1 tablespoon palm* or Demerara sugar

70 g macadamia nuts, toasted

3 large, mild red chillies, chopped

1 teaspoon finely chopped lemongrass stalk

1 tablespoon soy sauce

MAKES ABOUT 250 ML

*see glossary pages 140–141

This is a variation on the popular peanut satay sauce. It's good with barbecued kebabs, meat or vegetable, especially sweet potato ones.

Heat the oil in a small saucepan over medium heat. Add the blachan and gently fry for 1 minute, breaking it up with a wooden spoon. Add the garlic and shallots and sauté for 3 minutes.

Add the coconut cream and sugar and bring to the boil, then reduce to a simmer for 1 minute.

Put the macadamia nuts, chillies, lemongrass and soy sauce in a blender or small food processor and blend in bursts, adding the coconut cream mixture a little at a time until well combined.

The sauce will keep in the refrigerator for up to 3 days.

tomato and coconut curry sauce

1 tablespoon groundnut oil

1 onion, very finely chopped

4 tablespoons very finely chopped coriander stems and roots

3-cm piece of fresh ginger, peeled and minced

2 tablespoons red curry paste

420-g tin chopped tomatoes

¼ teaspoon sea salt

200 ml coconut cream

1 tablespoon Thai fish sauce*

MAKES ABOUT 500 ML

see glossary pages 140–141

This rich Thai-style tomato sauce is wonderful as a spooning sauce to spice up barbecued foods. The recipe uses only the stems and roots of the coriander. You can scatter the leaves over as a garnish or reserve for another use.

Heat the oil in a saucepan over medium to low heat. Add the onion, coriander, ginger and red curry paste and cook for about 10 minutes until soft and fragrant.

Stir in the tomatoes and salt and simmer for 20 minutes until thick. Stir in the coconut cream and fish sauce and gently heat.

The sauce will keep for up to 3 days in the refrigerator.

walnut, mint and yoghurt sauce

1 thick slice of day-old white bread

1 garlic clove, crushed

freshly squeezed juice of 1 lemon

70 g walnuts, chopped

3 tablespoons olive oil

150 ml thick natural yoghurt

leaves from a small bunch of mint, finely chopped

sea salt

MAKES ABOUT 250 ML

This unusual spooning sauce, made with ground walnuts, bread, yoghurt and mint, is delicious with lamb, chicken or vegetables.

Put the bread in a heat-proof bowl and pour over boiling water. When cool enough to handle, squeeze out the excess water with your hands.

Put the bread in a food processor with the garlic, lemon juice and walnuts and process to a paste. While the motor is running, add the oil. Transfer to a bowl and fold in the yoghurt and mint. Season to taste with salt. For a thinner dipping sauce, fold through a little water.

The sauce will keep for up to 3 days in the refrigerator.

glossary of ingredients

Apple syrup
New Zealand's alternative to real maple syrup, apple syrup is made from 100 per cent orchard-fresh apples, with no added sugar or preservatives, the flavour is tart, crisp and clean. Apple's natural affinity with so many foods makes it a versatile staple, and once you discover its many uses, it may become indispensable. If you can't find it, a clear, runny honey may be substituted.

Blachan
This is a pungent, dark-brown, dried shrimp paste. It is an essential ingredient in South-east Asian cooking, particularly Thai food, and is used in very small amounts in soups and curries. It is sold in tins or jars, or as hard slabs or cakes. You will find it at Asian grocers, specialist online retailers and larger supermarkets.

Bhuja mix
Similar to the popular snack food Bombay Mix, bhuja is an all-natural spicy mixture of peanuts and crisped rice. It is now stocked in most larger supermarkets.

Chaat masala
This is an Indian spice mix. It has a fresh, clean taste with tart notes and is traditionally used with fruit- and vegetable-based salads. It is also ideal used as a dry rub to flavour vegetables before cooking. You will find it at Asian grocers and some specialist online retailers.

Chinese five-spice powder
A pungent mixture of five dried spices commonly used in Chinese cookery, this brown powder is made of ground star anise, fennel seeds, cloves, cassia, cinnamon and Sichuan peppercorns. It is available from Chinese grocers, specialist online retailers and some larger supermarkets.

Curry leaves
Dried curry leaves have almost no flavour to them, but fresh leaves, when bruised, are extremely aromatic. They give off an intense spicy aroma with a citrus note and have a warm, pleasant and lemony taste that is faintly bitter. Although available as dried leaves, it is much better to buy curry leaves fresh from Indian grocers, where they may be labelled 'meetha neem' or 'kari patta'.

Edamame beans
A relative newcomer to the food scene, the edamame (or soya bean) originated in China and is popular in Japan. Soya beans have been used for many years in food manufacture and as a meat alternative for vegetarians. However, this humble bean is now being hailed as a new superfood and is said to be the only vegetable to contain all nine amino acids. As such, it is a complete protein source like meat or eggs. It is also high in fibre, vitamin C and folic acid and helps lower cholesterol. It looks something like a cross between a broad bean and a pea. They beans are now available in some supermarkets and most health food shops.

Harissa paste
This fiercely hot chilli purée comes from North Africa, where it is used extensively as a condiment and diluted with stock, water or fresh tomato sauce to flavour couscous, soups and tagines (stews). Moroccan food is growing in popularity so harissa paste is now widely available in supermarkets, but if you can't find it, you can make an adequate substitute. Simply, replace 2 tablespoons harissa paste with 1 tablespoon crushed red chilli paste blended with 1 crushed garlic clove and ¼ teaspoon ground coriander.

Japanese aubergines
These are most commonly purple, but can range in colour from lavender to pink, green and white as well. They are thin-skinned with a delicate flavour and fewer of the bitter-tasting seeds found in other aubergine varieties. Look for an aubergine that is relatively light for its size, firm, with dark-coloured, smooth, shiny skin. It is fine to substitute standard aubergines if you can't find them.

Japanese mayonnaise
This is a richer, more creamy and flavoursome mayonnaise than the standard British types. It is made with rice vinegar instead of distilled vinegar, so that it complements Japanese food. It is sold in squeezy plastic screw-top bottles and is available at Japanese shops and specialist online retailers. If you can't find it, ordinary mayonnaise can be substituted.

Japanese seven-spice powder
This intriguing spice mix features no less than seven dried and ground flavours – red pepper flakes, Sichuan peppercorns, tiny flakes of mandarin orange peel, black hemp seeds (or white poppy seeds), nori seaweed and white sesame seeds. It loses its aroma quickly, so is best bought in small quantities. It's available from Japanese shops or specialist online retailers.

Japanese soy sauce
There are several types of Japanese soy sauce, all of them rather different in character from Chinese soy sauces, so it is best to use these when cooking any Japanese-style dish. Usukuchi soy sauce is light in colour and tastes less salty than Chinese light soy sauce, and is a good choice for the recipes in this book. Tamari is dark and thick with a strong flavour, and is even less salty than the light type. Shoyu is a full-flavoured sauce that is aged for up to two years. In between there is the very popular Kikkoman, which is a brand name and the equivalent of the Chinese regular soy sauce. It is available from Japanese shops and specialist online retailers. If you can't find it, subsitute Chinese light (or golden) soy sauce.

Kaffir lime leaves
Although these leaves have an unmistakable citrus smell, they actually belong to a subspecies of the citrus family – a tree that is native to South-east Asia. The leaves are used extensively in the cuisines of Thailand, Indonesia and Malaysia, where they are torn or finely shredded and added to sweet-and-sour soups and curries. It is best to buy them freeze-dried for maximum freshness and taste. You will find them at Asian grocers, some supermarkets and specialist online retailers.

Micro greens (sprouts)
Small in size but big in flavour, micro greens are the latest must-have addition to any salad. Used to flavour or garnish, they are quite simply the shoots of regular salad plants (like celery, beetroot and radish) harvested just after they have developed their first tiny leaves. Not only is the taste more intense than when the leaves reach maturity, but you can also raise your own nutritious crop in only 7–10 days and all you need is a moderately sunny windowsill!

Mirin
This is a sweet cooking sake from Japan with a light, delicate flavour and a low alcohol content. Mirin is normally stirred into dishes during the final stages of cooking so that it does not lose its light flavour. It adds a mild sweetness to sauces or dips. Combined

with soy sauce, it is the basis of teriyaki sauce, which is popular for basting grilled foods. It is available from Japanese shops, some larger supermarkets and specialist online retailers. If you can't find it, dry sherry makes a reasonable substitute.

Nigella seeds

These tiny black seeds have little aroma, but when rubbed in between the fingers they give off a peppery smell. They have a herb-like taste, similar to oregano and are widely used in Indian cooking – in lentil dhals and vegetable dishes and sprinkled over naan bread. Black cumin is sometimes mistaken for nigella seeds but it is not the same thing. You will find them at Indian grocers and specialist online retailers.

Orzo pasta

Orzo is an Italian word that literally translates as 'barley', but in common culinary usage, orzo is understood to mean rice-shaped pasta slightly smaller than a pine nut. It is frequently used in soups. Despite its rice shape, orzo is not made out of rice but of hard wheat semolina and makes a great alternative to rice in both salads and warm dishes. It is available from Italian delis, larger supermarkets or specialist online retailers.

Palm sugar

This sugar was originally made from the sugary sap of the palmyra palm or date palm. Now it is also made from the sap of the sago and coconut palms and may be called coconut sugar. It is a golden brown paste, sold in cakes, blocks, tins or even tubes. It may be light- or dark-coloured, soft and gooey or hard. It is a key ingredient in Thai food and is often used to sweeten savoury dishes to balance out the salt flavour of fish. I prefer to

buy it in cake form and chop it so that it can be measured in teaspoons. It is available from specialist online retailers. If you can't find it, simply substitute an equal amount of golden or unrefined caster sugar.

Pomegranate molasses

This thick, fragrant and gloriously tangy reduction of pomegranate juice is made by boiling the liquid until it becomes sticky and syrupy. It is an essential ingredient in traditional Middle Eastern cooking and has become increasingly popular over the last few years. It is available from larger supermarkets and specialist online retailers.

Preserved lemons

These are used extensively in North African cooking, especially in savoury dishes such as tagines (spicy stews) and salads. Whole lemons are packed in jars with salt. The interesting thing with preserved lemons is that you eat only the rind, which contains the essential flavour of the lemon, rather than the flesh. It has an intense flavour and can really lift a dish. The lemons are available from specialist online retailers.

Quinoa

Hailed as the supergrain of the future, quinoa (pronounced keen-wa) is actually a grain of the past as it was grown by the Incas for hundreds of years. The tiny, bead-shaped grains have a mild, slightly bitter taste and firm texture. They are cooked in the same way as rice, but the grains quadruple in size, becoming almost translucent. It is growing in popularity and is readily available in health-food shops, larger supermarkets and specialist online retailers.

Rice stick noodles

Rice noodles are more common than wheat noodles in southern

China. Like wheat noodles they come in various widths, from the very thin strands known as rice vermicelli to rice sticks, which start at around 2 mm and can be as wide as 1 cm. A wide range of dried rice noodles is available in Asian or Chinese grocers, and fresh ones can be found in the chilled cabinets. Most supermarkets will stock a limited range.

Rice vinegars

The vinegar fermented from rice is dark amber in colour and is referred to in China as red or black vinegar. Vinegar distilled from rice grains is clear, so it is called white vinegar. Rice vinegar is an important ingredient for Chinese sweet-and-sour and hot-and-sour sauces, and is added to many other dishes to impart flavour. It is available from Chinese shops or larger supermarkets.

Sake

This is a Japanese alcoholic drink made from fermented rice. It is often referred to in English as Japanese rice wine (see also Mirin). It is available from Japanese shops and specialist online retailers.

Sev

These delicate, deep-fried crispy noodles from India are made with chickpea flour and make a great addition to salads. You can buy them at most Indian grocers.

Sichuan peppercorns

Also known as anise pepper, this spice is not actually a part of the pepper family but the ground husks of berries from the prickly ash tree, common to the Sichuan region of China. It has a pungent aroma with a hint of citrus and is one of the spices in both Chinese five-spice powder and Japanese seven-spice powder. It is available from Chinese grocers,

larger supermarkets and specialist online retailers.

Sumac

This increasingly popular spice grows wild, but is also cultivated in Italy, Sicily and throughout the Middle East. It is widely used in Lebanese, Syrian, Turkish and Iranian cooking. The red berries have an astringent quality, with a pleasing sour-fruit flavour. They are used whole, but ground sumac is available from Middle Eastern grocers or specialist online retailers.

Tahini

This thick, oily paste is made with ground sesame seeds and is a key ingredient in the Middle Eastern chickpea dip, hummus. It is now readily available in most supermarkets and health-food shops.

Thai fish sauce

This sauce is a fermentation of small, whole fish (sometimes prawns) and is quite salty, so a little goes a long way. It is an essential ingredient in Thai cooking, and because of the growing popularity of South-east Asian cuisines in the West, it has become a staple storecupboard ingredient. It is widely distributed and most supermarkets stock it.

Verjuice

This derives from the phrase 'green juice' and was widely used in the Middle Ages. Having fallen from favour, it is now experiencing a fashionable revival. It is usually a sour, acidic juice extracted from unripened grapes and therefore is often produced by wine makers, especially in France, Australia and Spain. If you aren't able to find it in your supermarket, do try specialist online retailers, as it is worth the effort. You can use freshly squeezed lemon juice as a substitute.

index

websites

specialist ingredients

Seasoned Pioneers
www.seasonedpioneers.co.uk
Tel: 0800 068 2348 (Freephone)
This innovative company sources and sells authentic, specialist seasonings. Highly commended by many leading food writers and chefs, they source and sell spice mixes from each corner of the globe. Range includes Chinese five-spice powder and sumac.

www.thespiceshoponline.com
Tel: 020 7221 4448
This delightful shop in Notting Hill sells a wide range of herbs, spice blends, nuts and dried fruit, including home-made preserved lemons.

Gourmet House
www.gourmet.house.co.uk
A small shop with a big passion for food. Buy Indian, Chinese and Thai ingredients online, including palm sugar, Thai basil and kaffir lime leaves.

Brindisa
www.brindisa.com
All things Spanish, including beans and pulses, charcuterie, cheese, tinned fish, honey, oils and vinegars, olives and rice.

Maroque
www.maroque.co.uk
Authentic Moroccan ingredients, such as preserved lemons and harissa paste, available to buy online.

Shop New Zealand
www.shopnewzealand.co.nz
Delivering gourmet New Zealand products around the world, including apple syrup and macadamia oil.

Carluccio's
www.carluccio's.com
Quality Italian produce, cured goods, pasta, grain and condiments, plus a fabulous deli selling quality antipasti and Italian cheeses.

quality produce

Abel & Cole
www.abel-cole.co.uk
Organic fruit and vegetable delivery throughout the UK, with a focus on British seasonal produce.

M.Moen & Sons
www.moen.co.uk
Top-quality free-range and organic meats, plus a well-stocked deli.

Loch Fyne
www.loch-fyne.com
High-quality seafood, meat and game by mail order.

Neal's Yard Dairy
www.nealsyarddairy.co.uk
British and Irish cheeses, kept in excellent condition. Branches across the UK, plus mail order.

kitchen equipment

Lakeland
www.lakeland.co.uk
Tel: 015394 88100
Huge range of cookware and kitchen equipment, including vegetable peelers, salad spinners and lettuce knives.

John Lewis
www.johnlewis.co.uk
Wide range of cookware, kitchen equipment and tableware, including attractive salad bowls and servers.

grow your own

The Herb Farm
www.theherbfarm.co.uk
Marvellous selection of live herb plants delivered to your door, including numerous varieties of oregano and rosemary.

Seeds of Italy
www.seedsofitaly.com
Real Italian seeds supplied mail order for growing your own Italian fruit, vegetables and herbs.

The following recipes were originally published in New Zealand by *Cuisine* magazine, a Fairfax publication.

Page 85 (*issue 109, March 2005*)
Page 136, bottom (*issue 111, July 2005*)
Pages 16, 36, 82 (*issue 120, January 2007*)
Page 51 (*issue 122, May 2007*)
Pages 40, 43, 44 and 47 (*issue 125, January 2008*)